· I USED TO BE ·
PERFECT

I USED TO BE

PERFECT

A Study of Sin and Salvation

George R. Knight

2nd Edition

ANDREWS UNIVERSITY PRESS
BERRIEN SPRINGS, MICHIGAN

Copyright © 2001 by Andrews University Press
213 Information Services Building
Berrien Springs, MI 49104-1700
Telephone: (269) 471-6134; FAX: (269) 471-6224
Email: info@andrewsuniversitypress.com
Website: www.andrewsuniversitypress.com

Unless otherwise noted, Bible texts in this book are from the
Revised Standard Version of the Bible.

ISBN 1-883925-31-2

Library of Congress Control Number 2001094416

Printed in the United States of America

08 07 06 05   6 5 4 3

"There is scarce any expression in holy writ, which has given more offense than this. The word *perfect* is what many cannot bear. The very sound of it is an abomination to them."

John Wesley

"'You have heard that it was said, "You shall love your neighbor and hate your enemy." But I say to you, Love your enemies and pray for those who persecute you, *so that you may be sons of your Father who is in heaven*; for he makes his sun rise on the evil and on the good, and sends rain on the just and on the unjust. For if you love those who love you, what reward have you? Do not even the tax collectors do the same? And if you salute only your brethren, what more are you doing than others? Do not even the Gentiles do the same? *You, therefore, must be perfect, as your heavenly Father is perfect.*'"

Jesus

"The last day will show who is right and who is wrong [in the understanding of holiness or perfection]. In the meantime, I am quite certain that to exhibit bitterness and coldness towards those who cannot conscientiously work with us is to prove ourselves very ignorant of real holiness."

J. C. Ryle

Dedication

to Fallon Knight
Grandson Extraordinaire

May Jesus
Be Special in Your Life
Is My Prayer

Contents

A Word to the Reader

Sin and salvation. Those two words stand at the very center of what Christianity is all about, with the first focusing on the human problem and the second on God's solution.

While it is true that those words are central to the meaning of Christianity, it is also true that they have been some of the most misunderstood words in the history of the church. It was so in my case. For years I struggled through a series of false conceptions on those most important topics. In the process I frustrated not only my own life, but the lives of those who had to associate with me.

This slender volume represents the core of my thinking on the topic. Each chapter seeks to move beyond the surface into the deeper meaning of the topic and on to its outworking in daily Christian experience.

The first chapter takes up the problem of SIN and its relationship to sins. That topic is all important, since, of necessity, an adequate doctrine of salvation must be based on an adequate understanding of SIN. The second chapter deals with the concept of LAW and how God's laws relate to the eternal underlying principle of LAW. One of the greatest tragedies of Christian history is that men and women have sought to keep the laws without keeping the LAW. The third chapter examines justification as the work of a lifetime and sanctification as the work of a moment. It focuses on not only the deeper meaning of those two words but also on what they mean for daily Christian living.

Chapter four highlights the difference between the basic TEMPTATION and all of its offspring, which show up as temptations. Once again, it is speaking to a topic widely misunderstood in the Christian community. The fifth chapter treats SINLESS-NESS and PERFECTION from a biblical perspective and seeks to move our understanding beyond the error of interpreting those concepts from our twenty-first-century point of view and vocabulary. Only as we comprehend how the Bible uses the words can we come to a Christian understanding of them. The final chapter utilizes a bit of my personal journey in the realm of perfectionism to illustrate points that have been treated in previous chapters.

Five of the six chapters in *I Used to Be Perfect* were first delivered to the Annual Council of the General Conference of Seventh-day Adventists in October 1992. The sixth (chapter 5) was added when the series was presented at the North New South Wales camp meeting in Australia in October 1993. Because they first were developed as oral presentations, these chapters still have some of the hallmarks of oral style, including a bit of repetition.

The present volume is the culmination of four books that led up to it. *From 1888 to Apostasy: The Case of A. T. Jones* (1987) and *Angry Saints: Tensions and Possibilities in the Adventist Struggle over Righteousness by Faith* (1989) dealt with aspects of God's plan of salvation in Adventist history. *My Gripe with God: A Study in Divine Justice and the Problem of the Cross* (1990), on the other hand, began to treat the topic theologically. That book focuses on what God has done *for* us. It was followed by *The Pharisee's Guide to Perfect Holiness: A Study of Sin and Salvation* (1992), which deals with what God does *in* us. *I Used to Be Perfect* builds upon concepts laid out in those four volumes and in some ways moves beyond them in conceptualization and in applying the material to the meaning of daily life. The much more extensive *Pharisee's Guide*, however, treats many of the topics in greater depth and with more sophistication.

A Word to the Reader

The present edition of *I Used to Be Perfect* differs in several ways from the first edition (published in 1994). The most significant difference is the inclusion of study questions at the end of each chapter. They were added to make the volume more useful to study groups and for those who choose to use it in the university and college classroom. It is, in fact, that latter group that has stimulated the publication of this second edition. Another improvement over the first edition is the addition of footnotes and scripture and content indexes.

I would like to express my appreciation to Susan Robinson of Pacific Press Publishing Association for transcribing these sermons from the original tape recordings; to Bonnie Beres, my secretary, for making the seemingly endless rounds of corrections and refinements as the first edition went to press, and also for her work on the second edition; to Ronald Knott and Deborah Everhart for guiding the second edition through the publication process; and to the administration of Andrews University for providing financial support and time for research and writing.

I trust that *I Used to Be Perfect: A Study of Sin and Salvation* will be a blessing to its readers as they seek to gain a better understanding of God's great plan of salvation.

George R. Knight
Andrews University
June 5, 2001

CHAPTER ONE

Sin is Love

Eating cheese is not SIN!

I figured most of you would agree with me on that point.

So I'll see if I can antagonize the rest of you.

Eating rats, snakes, snails, or even hogs is not SIN.

Sabbath breaking is not SIN.

Murder is not SIN.

Theft is not SIN.

SIN is prior to all these things. They may be sins—maybe—but they are not SIN.

SIN is love.

Earth's first SIN

Perhaps we can best understand the nature of SIN by looking at the first sin in Genesis 3, the original sin by Eve. The essential question is, "Did Eve sin when she took the fruit or before she took the fruit?" The answer will help us come to grips with the nature of both SIN and sins. Now, let's go to the biblical record.

The first part of Genesis 3 centers around the dynamics of temptation. "The serpent," we read, "was more subtle than any other wild creature that the Lord God had made. He said to the woman, 'Did God say...?'" (Gen. 3:1). When Satan comes to me, when he comes to you, his first point of attack is to get us to question the Word of God—to get us to doubt whether God said it. If the devil can win the battle at that point, he has won the war.

However, that's not usually the end, because often Satan doesn't win there. And so the passage goes on in verse 2: "And the woman said to the serpent, 'We may eat of the fruit of the trees of the garden; but God said, "You shall not eat of the fruit of the tree which is in the midst of the garden, neither shall you touch it, lest you die."'" But the serpent replied to the woman, "You certainly don't believe that, do you? You won't die" (see verse 4). So if the first point in Satan's strategy is to get us to doubt God's Word (to tempt us to doubt that God said it), the second point is to get us to doubt that God means what He says.

And the passage goes on, "'For God knows that when you eat of it your eyes will be opened, and you will be like God, knowing good and evil.' So...the woman saw that the tree was good for food, and that it was a delight to the eyes, and that the tree was to be desired to make one wise" (Gen. 3:5, 6). The third step in temptation is to get us to doubt God's good intentions toward us. Underlying this step is the idea that God wants to keep us from the good things of life—that He doesn't want us to be happy. Thus He can't be trusted.

or that these laws still relate to us today.

Even though God made us to enjoy life to the fullest, Satan comes and says:

- "God can't be trusted."
- "Doubt God's Word."
- "Doubt whether God means it."
- "Doubt the goodness of His intentions."

If one listens to the tempter, the natural conclusion is that God can't be trusted. Therefore, do your own thing. And that is exactly what Eve did in verse 6. The Bible says she took of the fruit and she ate it. She took. But note. Something happened in Eve's head or in her heart before she took the fruit. By the time she had taken the fruit, she had already sinned. In essence, she had told God to leave her alone, that she knew better than He did what was good for her. She had rejected His Word and will and replaced it with her own wisdom and will. In short, before reaching for the fruit, Eve had chosen her own will over the will of God. She had put her self on the throne of her life, at the center of her universe, thus displacing God. In actuality, she had focused her love on her self rather than on God. And that is the core of SIN.

Eve committed SIN when she loved herself and her desire more than she loved God and His will. She committed SIN in her heart. And that SIN in her heart led to the taking and the eating of the fruit. SIN in the heart leads to sins in terms of action. Something happens in the heart first. First, there is SIN in the heart. That SIN in the heart then gives birth to sinful actions. Thus:

SIN → sins

Now up to the point of Genesis 3:6, Adam and Eve had been safe in Jesus. But with the entrance of SIN into their lives, there was a major ground shift. They were no longer safe in Him. They had become lost.

The consequences of SIN immediately follow in Genesis 3:7. First, Adam and Eve have a terrible feeling of *nakedness*. That's a technicolor word. I like the Bible because it uses real words that appeal to our experience.

Have you ever felt naked? When I was a boy, I used to have a dream over and over. It was always the same dream, and it always took place at the local swimming pool. Everybody had a bathing suit; that is, everybody but me. What an uncomfortable feeling! And I always used to scramble to hide behind something—like the walls of the shower room. But dreams are miraculous things. The walls would disappear. There was no way to escape from my nakedness.

Likewise, when SIN entered, Adam and Eve got an uncomfortable "naked" feeling—a feeling of disturbing and inescapable guilt. That gut-level feeling had many results. One of them was fig leaves. The Bible tells us that Adam and Eve sought to cover their nakedness (guilt) with fig leaves. Have you ever tried to cover your nakedness with fig leaves? It's not a very satisfactory solution. Try it sometime, and you will see what I mean. Fig leaves in Genesis 3 signify humans seeking to cover their own nakedness through their own effort. Fig leaves signify Adam and Eve trying to solve their own guilt problem. Fig leaves represent salvation by works.

A second result of sin is a fearful discomfort with God, reflecting a broken relationship with Him (Gen. 3:8). Adam and Eve are now afraid of their Maker. They hide from God.

Unfortunately, broken relationships with God lead to broken relationships with other people. Whenever humans are out of tune with God, they will be alienated from each other. Thus when God questions Adam about his part with the fruit, Adam immediately blames Eve. "It's not my fault," claims Adam; "it's her fault. She gave me the fruit." Such is the record of the end of harmony in earth's only perfect marriage. "She did it," "He did it," "It's your fault" have ever since echoed down the corridors of marital history. Disharmony with God brought disharmony with other people in its train (see Gen. 3:11, 12).

Another consequence of sin is a broken relationship with one's self. That is reflected in Eve's inability to confess her part in the fall. Disclaiming any personal responsibility (as had Adam previously), she blames her problem on the devil: "The serpent beguiled me, and I ate" (Gen. 3:13)—"The devil made me do it." Humans despise confessing their own sins, but they love talking about their neighbor's sins, their pastor's sins, their husband's/wife's sins, their children's sins—anybody's sins but their own. Most people seem to genuinely enjoy confessing other people's sins, but steer clear of any admission of their own. Unfortunately, it is when we "confess our sins, [that] he...will forgive our sins and cleanse us from all unrighteousness" (1 John 1:9). "The heart is deceitful above all things" (Jer. 17:9). Since Eden, humans have lived in an alienated and fractured world.

After Genesis 3, Adam and Eve are no longer safe in Jesus. After the fall, they live as broken people in a broken world, and, unfortunately, the brokenness does not stop in Genesis 3. That is the significance of the Cain and Abel story with its brother murdering brother in Genesis 4. The brokenness goes on and on and on. Something happened to the human race in Genesis 3 that has not stopped.

We get some perspective on the problem by going back to the creation of humanity. In Genesis 1:26, 27, we read that Adam was created in the image and likeness of God; but in Genesis 5:3, we are told that Adam "became the father of a son in his *own* likeness, after his image." Adam's children were like Adam rather than like God. Ellen White puts it nicely when she says that all human beings since Adam have a "bent" toward evil.[1] And the apostle Paul tells us that SIN came into the world through one man (Rom. 5:12).

SIN is universal. There is one thing we never have to teach anyone—how to sin. Everything else has to be taught. How to sin comes naturally. Furthermore, every nation, every community, needs its police and its armed forces. Since Eden, there are no Shangri-Las, no heavens on earth. Since Eden, since SIN, we live east of Eden (Gen. 3:24).

The Bible does not tell us how the "bentness" to SIN is passed from one generation to the next, but we have empirical proof of the universal bentness among humans. While the personal guilt of Adam's sin is his alone, every child of Adam is born with a tendency to SIN. That tendency comes to fruition when a

17

young person becomes old enough to consciously choose his or her own will above the will of God.

SIN versus sins

Now back to Eve. Her act of eating was not the SIN, but the result of SIN already ruling in her heart. She fell before she took the fruit. She fell when she placed love for something (the fruit) and someone (herself) before her love for God.

SIN is love. SIN is *agapē* love—that special kind of God-like love that is central to the New Testament. In Luke 11:43 Jesus condemns the Pharisees because they had love (*agapaō*) for the best seats in the synagogue. Likewise, in 2 Timothy 4:10 we are told that Demas left the Christian way when he fell "in love" (*agapaō*) with this present world. Similarly, in 1 John 2:15 we are admonished not to "love [*agapaō*] the world or the things in the world." Such do not have the love of the Father in them. These passages do not say that there is anything wrong with the world, but they do teach us that to put anything in God's place is wrong.

SIN is love focused on the wrong object. SIN is to love the object more than the Creator of the object. It makes no difference whether that object is an external thing, another person, or one's own self. To love anything or anyone more than God is SIN. SIN is love aimed at the wrong target accompanied by a way of life lived in the direction of that aim. Thus we have SIN, which leads to sins.

SIN → sins

Some of my friends call this approach to SIN the "new theology." I would like to suggest that it might better be called the "new theology of the Sermon on the Mount." Jesus was in harmony with the explanation of SIN that I have presented. He made that plain when He said, "What comes out of the mouth proceeds from the heart, and this defiles a man. For out of the heart come evil thoughts, murder, adultery, fornication, theft," and so on

18

(Matt. 15:18,19). Again, in Matthew 12 Jesus noted that "out of the abundance of the heart the mouth speaks. The good man out of his good treasure brings forth good, and the evil man out of his evil treasure brings forth evil" (verses 34, 35).

The Bible pictures SIN as a relational concept. SIN is a way we relate to God. SIN at its most basic level is not some impersonal evil or residual animal behavior or bad trait built into human character. Rather, it is rebellion against the God of the universe (Isa. 1:2-4; Hos. 7:13). SIN is personal rather than impersonal. "Against thee, thee only, have I sinned," says the psalmist (Psalm 51:4). SIN is a personal attack against God's authority. "The flesh" (unconverted human nature), writes Paul, "is hostile to God" (Rom. 8:7). The sinner is an enemy of God (Rom. 5:10). An enemy is not just someone who simply falls short of doing someone else good. An enemy is in the opposite camp. Sinners actively work against God.

Beyond being personal, SIN is moral. It is a deliberate act of the will in rebellion against God. Thus Herbert Douglass can correctly say that "sin is a created being's clenched fist in the face of his Creator; sin is the creature distrusting God, deposing Him as the Lord of his life."[2] And in like manner, Emil Brunner can claim that sin "is like the son who strikes his father's face in anger,...it is the bold self-assertion of the son's will above that of the father."[3]

Sinful acts versus sinful nature

The crucial point to recognize is that SIN is much more than a series of unrelated actions. It reflects a state of heart and mind. The first element in salvation is recognizing that we are sinners. That means much more than recognizing that I commit sins "a," "b," and "c." "It means," writes Edward Vick, "acknowledging that we are the kind of people who do such things.... To recognize that we are sinners means that we recognize there is a power that lords it over us and prevents us from being what God

19

intends us to be."[4] That power, says Paul, is "the power of sin" (Rom. 3:9). It is the "power of sin" that too many underestimate when they talk about SIN. Thus they think that they can over-come SIN through overcoming sin "a" and sin "b" and sin "c." The problem central to that procedure is that after sins "a," "b," and "c" are cared for, we still remain sinners.

Many of us have *personally*—and I'll emphasize that word because I'm one—discovered that the SIN problem is not solved in our lives by mere external tinkering, in spite of our dedication and all the effort we may expend. We can leave off doing "bad" things and still be essentially selfish and mean, or, worse yet, proud—proud of our goodness.

The Bible saves its most dreadful words for describing the condition of sinners. It describes sinful humans in terms of bondage, slavery, servitude, and a process of degeneracy that cannot be reversed without God's intervention. Humanity is "dead in sin" and "lost." Ellen White is much of the same mind. She notes that the "heart of man is by nature cold and dark and unloving."[5] "By nature," she writes, "the heart is evil."[6] Even though Adam originally had a well-balanced mind and pure thoughts, "through disobedience, his powers were perverted, and selfishness took the place of love."[7] Again she notes, while talking about Luke 18 and the prayer of the self-righteous Pharisee, "Of all sins," that of "pride and self-sufficiency" is "the most hopeless, the most incurable."[8] The problem is that when I am good—when I think I'm good—I feel no need of Christ.

Different views of sin lead to different paths to salvation

The point I want to make and that I've been driving at as the foundation of this book is that an inadequate doctrine of SIN will of necessity lead to an inadequate doctrine of salvation. This is one of the most important understandings in Christian life. It's no accident that the theological war in Adventism is over the doctrine of SIN. Many people may not consciously recognize that fact, but the doctrine of sin inevitably stands at the foundation of the struggle over how people are saved. If we are going to understand how people are saved, we need to understand what they are being saved from. The beginning place for discussing salvation is an understanding of SIN, because the cure must be of equal magnitude to the disease. The solution must be commensurate with the problem.

Seventh-day Adventists are in special danger in this whole realm because we have confused behavior and ethics with religion. And, worse yet, we are utterly confounded on the difference between the character of Christ and lifestyle issues.

My main point at this juncture is that *different views of SIN lead to radically different roads to salvation*. If sin is seen as a series of downward actions, as in the following illustration,

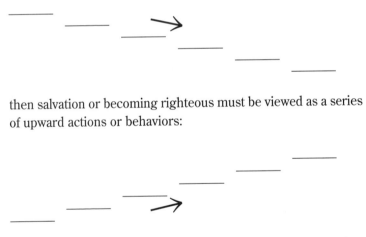

then salvation or becoming righteous must be viewed as a series of upward actions or behaviors:

According to this scheme, when all one's actions are in line with God's will and when all one's individual sins are overcome, that person is perfect and ready for translation.

Now that is a nice picture—maybe. But it's not the New Testament picture provided by Christ and Paul. To the contrary, the Pharisees perpetrate that view in the New Testament. The

New Testament's primary focus is on the level of SIN rather than on the level of sins. As a result, the New Testament speaks of becoming a Christian as a crucifixion and a rebirth, the receiving of a new heart and a new mind, a total transformation. Becoming a Christian is not a program of adding one virtue to another. Rather, it is one of complete transformation (Rom. 12:2).

Being saved is both accepting the death of Christ as our substitute *and* having our hearts transformed (that is, having our *agapē* love refocused from our self back to God and others). Such a new-birth experience implies—no, it demands—a ground shift in all that we do and all that we think. The New Testament teaches a transformational view of salvation rather than one of addition. Thus when a person gets Jesus, when one gets RIGHTEOUSNESS, when one accepts Christ's death and resurrection and puts God back at the center of his or her heart, the result will be righteous living, righteous actions. Such actions naturally flow out of an individual's new relationship to Jesus. Thus:

RIGHTEOUSNESS → righteous actions

People cannot have Jesus in their hearts, they cannot live the new and transformed life, without righteous living being demonstrated. Salvation is a unit. Being saved is choosing to put God and His will back into the center of our lives. It means leaving off our prideful rebellion, even pride in our goodness.

Pride in ones own goodness is absolute foolishness. Whatever 'good' one has achieved in his or her life has been a gift from*

Will you say "Yes" or "No" to God?

In closing this chapter, I would like to state that there are only two ways men and women can relate to God. We can say "Yes" to God and His will, or we can say "No" to God and His will. There are no other options. It's either a "Yes" to God or a "No" to God. Saying "Yes" to God is a FAITH relationship. Saying "No" to God is a SIN relationship. We are all related to God. There is no neutral ground. Neither is there a way of escape. We are either

God
*with an intended purpose that can quickly be wasted when you start to believe that it was something you did on your own,

22

saying "Yes" or we are saying "No" to the Creator of the universe. No moral creature can ignore God. By the very nature of things, we are forced into answering God with a "Yes" or a "No." And one of the most remarkable things in the universe is that God gives us the power of choice as the Holy Spirit works upon our wills. If I were God, I would have saved a whole lot of problems by never giving Lucifer, or you, such power. <u>One of the greatest powers in the universe is the power of the human will to say "Yes" or "No" to God.</u>

A human being's will, under the prodding unction of the Holy Spirit, determines his or her relationship to God. There are only two ways of relating to God—the SIN relationship and the FAITH relationship. As a result, I am either safe in Jesus, or I am out of Him and lost. There are no other options. Those electing to be in Christ have allowed God to reverse the effects of the fall in their lives. They have had their love refocused toward God and His will.

It should be noted, however, that just as SIN is love, so salvation is also love. Not only is salvation God's love in dying for us on the cross, but it means our love toward Him and toward others—a love that has been transformed and energized through the power of the Holy Spirit.

Points to ponder

1. You have been asked to give a 20-minute presentation to a youth group on SIN. What six descriptive points would form the basis of your outline?

2. Why is SIN more important than sins? What is the difference between the two?

3. Why is it that people who are out of harmony with God are also out of harmony with each other?

4. What makes the sin of goodness the most serious of all sins?

5. In what way is an understanding of SIN foundational to any discussion of salvation?

Notes

1. Ellen G. White, *Education* (Mountain View, CA: Pacific Press, 1952), 29.

2. Herbert E. Douglass, *Why Jesus Waits*, rev. ed. ([Riverside, CA]: Upward Way Publishers, 1987), 53.

3. Emil Brunner, *The Mediator*, trans. Olive Wyon (New York: Macmillan, 1934), 462.

4. Edward W. H. Vick, *Is Salvation Really Free?* (Washington, DC: Review and Herald, 1983), 86.

5. Ellen G. White, *Thoughts from the Mount of Blessing* (Mountain View, CA: Pacific Press, 1956), 21.

6. Ellen G. White, *The Desire of Ages* (Mountain View, CA: Pacific Press, 1940), 172.

7. Ellen G. White, *Steps to Christ* (Mountain View, CA: Pacific Press, 1958), 17.

8. Ellen G. White, *Christ's Object Lessons* (Washington, DC: Review and Herald, 1941), 154.

CHAPTER TWO

Adventists Neglect the LAW

Adventists neglect the LAW. As strange as it may seem—given our reputation as legalists—I have found in my forty years as an Adventist that one of our largest failings is neglect of the LAW of God. Even more astounding is the fact that the LAW is especially neglected by those who tend to emphasize the laws of God. I have found that those who have the most to say about the laws of God are all too often the ones most prone to neglect the LAW of God.

As Seventh-day Adventists, we love God's laws, and many of us get quite excited about such things as commandments and rules and regulations. Beyond that, we are justifiably exuberant when we glimpse ourselves in end-time prophecy in relationship to the commandments of God. "The dragon," we read in Revelation 12:17, "was angry with the woman, and went off to make war on the rest [remnant] of her offspring [seed]...who keep the commandments of God." That is a tremendous passage, particularly when it is viewed in the flow of prophetic history at the conclusion of the 1260 days, as reflected in verse 14.

And again we read, "Here is the patience of the saints [those who continue to wait for Jesus to come]: here are they that keep the commandments of God, and the faith of Jesus" (Rev. 14:12, KJV). Once again, that passage is in the flow of prophetic history.

ext..

Thus we read of the first angel, the second angel, the third angel, and then the great harvest at the end of the earth. Adventists have found genuine comfort in seeing themselves as God's end-time, commandment-keeping people.

LAW versus laws

Yes, Adventists have loved God's commandments and His rules and His laws and His regulations, but too often we have neglected His LAW in both rhetoric and practice. That was true at the Minneapolis General Conference session in 1888 as men became brutal with one another in defending the laws of God. Ellen White took great offense to that approach. She said of the delegates that if that is what their theology did to them, she wanted to get as far away from it as possible.[1]

Too often, we, as Seventh-day Adventists, have neglected the LAW of God. Just as we have been more interested in itemized sins and itemized righteousness, so we have been more interested in itemized laws than in God's basic LAW. Perhaps part of our problem is that Seventh-day Adventists are confused as to the nature of God's LAW.

I will never forget the shock I experienced when I discovered that the Ten Commandments were not the real LAW. In fact, in the context of universal history throughout eternity, the Ten Commandments might be viewed as a late development. One doesn't have to think too long or too hard to come to the conclusion that the law expressed in the Ten Commandments is neither eternal nor universal when we think in galactic terms. Take the fourth commandment, for example. It plainly states that the Sabbath was given as a memorial of the creation of our planet Earth. Even the seven-day cycle of twenty-four hours points to the creation of our planet and our solar system as the determinants of the Sabbath law found in the Decalogue. The Sabbath law in the Decalogue, however, does represent a universal and eternal principle that undergirds it. A similar analysis

26

could be done for some of the other specific commands in Exodus 20.

We find Ellen White to be in agreement with the line of thought that I'm setting forth. "The law of God," she penned, "existed before man was created. The angels were governed by it. Satan fell because he transgressed the principles of God's government.... After Adam's sin and fall nothing was taken from the law of God. The principles of the ten commandments existed before the fall, and were of a character suited to the condition of a holy order of beings."[2]

Let's go back to that quotation, because we're going to need an understanding of it as we move toward a better comprehension of character perfection. (Please realize that I am using building blocks. Chapter 1 dealt with SIN. This one covers LAW. They are related, like heads and tails of the same coin. We still have to get saved—that is chapter 3. We still have to go to the cross—that is chapter 4. And we still have to become sinless and perfect—those are our last two chapters.) Undergirding any theology of salvation and the cross and perfection are basic concepts. Two of those concepts are SIN and LAW. They stand at the foundation of a correct understanding of what the great controversy is all about.

I'm going to repeat Ellen White's quotation: "The principles of the ten commandments existed before the fall, and were of a character suited to the condition of a holy order of beings. After the fall, the principles of those precepts were not changed, but additional precepts were given to meet man in his fallen state."[3] Again she wrote, "The law of God existed before man was created. It was adapted to the condition of holy beings; even angels were governed by it. After the Fall, the principles of righteousness were unchanged."[4] But, Mrs. White penned in another connection, after Adam's transgression the principles of the law "were definitely arranged and expressed to meet man in his fallen condition."[5]

While the new "expression" and "arrangement" of the LAW after the fall undoubtedly included ceremonial aspects, it also included the negativization of the LAW. After all, can you imagine God going around to the holy angels and saying, "Now watch out that you don't commit adultery with any of your neighbors." I'm not even sure that angels are capable physiologically of committing adultery. And do you think God had to go around and tell the angels, "Now watch out you don't lust after your neighbor's wife, make sure you don't steal his or her belongings, and be sure to respect your father and mother?" Tell me—do angels have fathers and mothers?

The angels kept the LAW without knowing it, because it was written in the very fabric of their hearts (compare Heb. 8:10; 2 Cor. 3:3). "Love," we read, "is the great principle that actuates the unfallen beings."[6] Angels did not have to be told "Thou shalt not kill" or "Thou shalt not steal," because they were positively motivated from the heart to care for one another. Only after the entrance of sin with its shift of the focal point of love from God and others to one's self did the LAW have to be reformulated in negative terms for beings who were driven by selfishness and negative motivations.

The correct identification of the LAW behind the laws is of utmost importance, since any accurate discussion of righteousness and perfection depends upon a correct understanding of God's LAW.

The Old Testament has at least three laws—the moral, the civil, and the ceremonial. Beyond that, the books of Moses and even the entire Old Testament are referred to as "the law." Thus the word "law" in the Bible has many meanings.

In the New Testament, however, Jesus makes the nature of the LAW behind the laws crystal clear. When asked concerning the great commandment, Jesus replied, "'You shall love the Lord your God with all your heart, and with all your soul, and with all your mind. This is the great and first commandment. And a second is like it, You shall love your neighbor as yourself. On these two commandments depend all the law and the prophets'" (Matt. 22:37-40).

Paul and James agree with Jesus but point to a further reduction of the LAW to one basic precept. Thus Paul can say in Romans 13 that "love is the fulfilling of the law" (verse 10) and in Galatians 5 that "the whole law is fulfilled in one word, 'You shall love your neighbor as yourself'" (verse 14). James, meanwhile, not only is in harmony with Paul, but expresses the ultimate unity of the LAW. He writes that "whoever keeps the whole law but fails in one point has become guilty of all of it" (James 2:8, 10).

Characteristics of the LAW

The concept underlying these New Testament discussions of LAW has several facets. First, the LAW is unified. There are not many principles undergirding the LAW but one. At its most basic level, the LAW can be summed up in one word—"love." Please note, "love" is the same word that John used to sum up the character of God. In 1 John 4:8 we read that "God is love." Now that makes good sense if the LAW is a reflection of God's character. And remember that reflecting God's character is a crucial issue in Christianity, and it is certainly a crucial issue in Adventism. These concepts will help us when we examine character perfection in chapter 6. Remember, the LAW is a reflection of God's character, and God's character centers upon the characteristics of caring about and loving others, even when they don't deserve it.

The Bible does not stop with merely equating LAW and love and God's character. It also begins to spell out the meaning of love so that humans and other created beings can begin to see its meaning in concrete situations. For unfallen beings, one can think of the necessary law as having two parts—love to God and love to one another. After the fall, however, the law needed further explication because of the degeneracy of the human race. While there is substantial evidence in Genesis and early Exodus of the existence of the laws contained in the Ten Commandments before Sinai, God chose to formally expound the two great principles of the law as ten precepts when He founded the nation of Israel as His special covenant people.

The first four commandments are an explication of aspects of the principle of loving God, while the last six particularize specific ways of loving one's neighbors. Thus the progression of law from one LAW to two laws to ten laws might be illustrated in the following way:

LAW → laws

God has a basic LAW. Out of the principle of that LAW come laws. This is very closely related to what we said in the last chapter about SIN leading to sins:

SIN → sins

and RIGHTEOUSNESS leading to righteous actions:

RIGHTEOUSNESS → righteous actions

The point to remember is that the real scene of action in the great controversy is not at the level of sins, laws, or righteous acts. Rather, the action in the great controversy is at the level of SIN, LAW, and RIGHTEOUSNESS. The action in the great controversy is aimed at SIN as misdirected love, LAW as the great principle of God's character, and RIGHTEOUSNESS as a life lived in Christ in harmony with the great principle of God's kingdom. Sins, laws, and righteous acts are important, but only as the outflowing of SIN, LAW, and RIGHTEOUSNESS.

Along this line, it is of interest to note that the first three words in *Patriarchs and Prophets* and the last three words in *The Great Controversy*, with over three thousand pages in between, are the same three words. Have you ever noticed that before? When I wrote *My Gripe With God*, a book focused on the cross, I realized that fact for the first time. Ellen White begins and ends the Conflict of the Ages series with the words "God is love." That is the central issue in the great controversy. That is the issue that needs to be demonstrated to the universe. That is the core of God's character. That is the core of all upright character.

One of the foundational problems of New Testament Pharisaism was the atomization of SIN into a series of actions. The atomization of SIN is directly related to the atomization of LAW and RIGHTEOUSNESS. While Christians ought to understand the nature of sins, laws, and righteous acts, they must also comprehend SIN, LAW, and RIGHTEOUSNESS if they are to come to a biblical understanding of salvation and perfection. *Because the Pharisees of old did not understand SIN and LAW, they could not correctly understand RIGHTEOUSNESS. The entire New Testament stands against their misunderstandings.*

Beyond unity, a second aspect of biblical law is that it is essentially positive rather than negative. Jesus plainly indicated that negative religion is not sufficient when He told the story in Matthew 12 of the person who swept his life clean and put it in order but failed to fill it with vital, outgoing Christianity. The final condition of that person, claimed Jesus, was worse than in the beginning (verses 43-45). "A religion which consists in *thou shalt nots*," writes William Barclay, "is bound to end in failure."[7]

The essentially positive nature of biblical law is also seen in Jesus' dealing with the rich young ruler, who came to Him, saying, "Good Master, what good thing shall I do, that I may have eternal life?"

Jesus met him on his own ground, saying, "Don't do this and don't do that."

"Ah ha," the young man replied, "I have already stopped doing all those things. What else have You got?"

Jesus said, "Well, if you are really serious about this whole business, if you really want to be perfect, why don't you go out and sell what you have and fully serve your neighbor."

The young ruler wasn't expecting that kind of an answer. He liked the "limited realm" of righteousness where people stop doing things. He balked when Jesus pointed him to the "continuous realm" of righteousness where there is no limit and no end of really caring for other people.

Jesus had pointed beyond the negative ten to the positive law of love. That, of course, was more than the young ruler was ready to commit himself to. He felt relatively comfortable with the negative law. He was good at not doing this and that, but he was not ready for the unlimited reach of God's LAW into every area of his life (see Matt. 19:16-22).

I am personally very uncomfortable with this whole concept of being a Christian as Jesus explained it. I am a Pharisee by nature. I am very happy with negative approaches to law because I like to know where the limits are. I feel more comfortable when I can see the extent of my obligations. That brings me to the lesson of Peter in Matthew 18.

Peter was concerned about how many times he should forgive his neighbor. Peter was no dummy. He knew what the rabbis had to say on the topic. They had read the book of Amos. They had concluded that the Lord forgives three times, and the fourth time He lets sinners have it. Well, rabbinic logic suggested, you can't be more generous than God. Therefore, they concluded, three times should be the limit of human forgiveness.

Now Peter had recognized that Jesus was not a minimalist. So he doubled the rabbinic three forgivenesses and added one for good measure, coming to the conclusion that seven forgivenesses would be quite generous. And that is a lot of forgiveness, if you start thinking about it. If I backed into your car seven times in the next seven days in the church parking lot, you would think that seven is probably about six times too

32

many. But Christ bowled poor Peter over. He said, "Peter, Peter, not seven but 490." Try that sometime. By the time you get to 490, you'll not have a car. You will also have lost count (see Matt. 18:21, 22).

In actuality Peter was not asking "How much can I love my neighbor?" but "When can I stop loving my neighbor?" That's a very human question. I like that question. When can I stop loving my neighbor? That is where we are as natural people. When can I be pensioned off from all this niceness and give people what they deserve? I don't like grace. Grace is giving people what they don't deserve. I don't mind getting it, but I don't really like passing grace on to others.

Christ comes back with an answer as to when Peter can stop loving his neighbor. His answer is the terrible story about the two debtors. One man owes one hundred pennies, and the other owes ten thousand talents. The one hundred pennies equals one hundred days wages. That is a stiff debt but not impossible to pay. By way of contrast, ten thousand talents is an absolutely impossible debt to pay. In fact, it would take 160,000 years if one worked seven days per week. Yet the king by grace forgives that huge debt. But the forgiven man refuses to pass on the forgiveness to his fellow, who owes him one hundred pennies. As a result, the king's forgiveness is revoked. The punch line of the story is that sinners, who have been forgiven an impossible debt, must pass on God's mercy to their fellow humans, just as God has had mercy on them. Thus Peter learned that there is never a time when he could stop loving his neighbor or stop passing on God's grace (Matt. 18:23-35). The frightful fact is that there is no limit to Christian love. [1]

Like Peter, we are much more comfortable with the negative than the positive approach to law. We want to know when we have fulfilled our quota of goodness so we can relax and be our normal selves. The negative limits the scope of righteousness and makes it humanly manageable and achievable. Thus legalists of all

33

stripes must of necessity focus on the "thou shalt nots" and the "small sins." Continuous love of all of one's enemies is a goal beyond human reach.

Legalists love to talk about negative and minute behaviors. That thought reminds me of a woman that Bruce Johnston (a former president of the North Pacific Union Conference) once met. They were discussing the sin of David, when she said, "Well, some people have that problem. Mine's eating granola between meals." From one perspective, she had almost arrived at perfection. Unfortunately, that negative approach to law falls far short of the New Testament ideal.

There is a type of righteousness that picks on smaller and smaller units of action. The New Testament is the reverse. The Christian way is the endless righteousness expressed in caring for God and humanity that one finds summarized in the two great commandments. It was that very ideal that drove the rich young ruler (with his smaller-and-smaller mentality) away from Christ in utter frustration.

But we like to define sin as some small negative action, because anybody can overcome a habit if he or she tries hard enough. On the other hand, I have an impossible time loving all my neighbors all the time. I can get the victory over cheese, peanut butter, or "granola between meals" any old time, but it takes God's grace for me to love all my neighbors all the time, particularly when my neighbor is defined by Jesus in a manner that includes enemies. That takes empowering grace.

So we want to know the limits of love and Christian living, so that we can know when we have arrived. Human perverseness loves the merely negative approach to law because it limits the scope of righteousness. It makes it humanly achievable. Strangely, many think that an emphasis on the two great commandments is a watering down of the demands laid upon the Christian in daily living. Christ repeatedly demonstrated the opposite to be true. In those two commands, we read in *Selected*

Messages, "the length and breadth, the depth and height, of the law of God is comprehended."[8]

In the Sermon on the Mount, Jesus expounded on the principles of the law and began to demonstrate their far-reaching inner meaning. It is the "principles," Mrs. White noted, that "remain forever the great standard of righteousness."[9] The negative approach to religion stems from a negative approach to law. The world has seen too much negative religion. A young pastor once told me that for many people "the major qualification for being a Christian is the ability to say 'don't.'" Unfortunately, that caricature is all too true for many people who need to come to grips with a higher standard. It is a relatively simple thing for me to avoid theft, murder, or adultery compared to the unending challenge of caring for all my neighbors as myself.

The negative precepts of the Ten Commandments certainly inform me about aspects of love to God and my neighbor; but important as they are, they are only the tip of the LAW itself. One can never be saved or become perfect by not working on Sabbath or avoiding theft. In fact, no one will ever be saved because of what he or she has not done. Christianity is a positive, not a negative.

Whether we like it or not (and the Pharisees of old certainly did not like it), Jesus put the standard of righteousness higher than "normal" people care to reach. And most legalists are normal humans. In fact, it is their emphasis on human accomplishment that proves their normality. They have merely shifted their pride from human accomplishment in worldly endeavors to human accomplishment in spiritual things.

The LAW in daily life

OK, you may be thinking, you got your point across about the LAW being positive and unified. What you have said is good and helpful, but what does it mean for my life?

Well, I thought you would never ask. But I'm delighted that you have, because the practical application of the topic stands at the very center of Christian living.

How individual Christians relate to the law is not only important but complex. Paul says in 1 Timothy 1:8 that "the law is good, if...one uses it lawfully." He thus implies that the law is less than good if it is used improperly. I would like to suggest that one of the greatest dangers the Christian faces is the wrong use of God's law. Of course, we all know, I hope, that a person cannot come into a saving relationship with God through keeping the law. We also know that the function of God's law is to point out our sin (our nakedness) and thereby drive us to Christ for forgiveness and clothing. Beyond that, we are aware of the fact that the law provides us with both a standard for daily living and the standard of God's judgment. What we often fail to realize is that *we can be quite zealous in keeping God's laws while utterly and totally failing in keeping God's LAW.*

Let me illustrate my point by asking you a question. When do Seventh-day Adventists rejoice? Sundown Friday or sundown Saturday? I can ask that question anyplace in the world to an Adventist audience, and I always get the same response—kind of a gentle chuckle. They know what I'm talking about. Too many of us keep the Sabbath as if it were a penalty for being an Adventist rather than the high point of the week. We have the correct day, but too often we have lost the principle of the law of love and the relationship to the God of love that make the day meaningful. The Sabbath becomes a weekly burden rather than a weekly delight.

I think A. T. Jones in the 1890s was right when he said that there are three types of Christians as they relate to a day of worship. There are Sunday keepers, Saturday keepers, and Sabbath keepers. The distinction between the last two is crucial to note. Anyone can be a Saturday keeper. After all, it is the right day. But it takes the infilling of the Holy Spirit to be a Sabbath keeper.

Only in loving relationship to the God of the universe do we discover the true meaning of Sabbath. Keeping Saturday is right, but keeping Sabbath is spiritual.

To make my point another way, I could say that when the LAW of God is in our hearts it will be natural and normal to keep God's many laws. But the reverse is not true. One may keep God's many laws and still not be keeping God's LAW. That is, a person can have outward obedience but not have God's love in his or her heart. Or to put it yet another way, one can keep the right day but be as mean as the devil.

The predicament of outward obedience accompanied by a lack of inward Christianity is one of the most spiritually dangerous situations we can be in. After all, people who are deceived at that point may feel quite satisfied with themselves spiritually because they are doing what is right. Like the prodigal son's older brother, they may never "come to themselves" and see their true condition.

That was the problem with the Pharisees of old. Never forget that they sincerely kept the laws but broke the LAW and put Christ on the cross. There has traditionally been a spirit of meanness among those who focus on laws rather than on the LAW. That meanness is especially aimed at those who disagree with them theologically and/or who may not be as zealous as they are on particular laws or rules or regulations. The spirit is not new. Jesus had to face it. And Ellen White called it "the spirit of the Pharisees," "the spirit of Minneapolis."[10]

God's plea is for us to get our priorities right. He wants us to keep His LAW so that we can truly keep His laws. The order is absolutely essential and crucial. The correct order keeps us away from a legalistic bookkeeping approach to salvation that recreates God into the image of a first-century Pharisee. The point to remember is that if we are safe in Jesus, He will live out His life in us. That means that not only will our love be refocused from our self to God and others, but it means that the wellspring of God's love will undergird our every action. "'This is the covenant that I will make with the house of Israel after those days, says the Lord: I will put my laws into their minds, and write them on their hearts, and I will be their God, and they shall be my people'" (Heb. 8:10).

Christianity is not just an improvement on the old life. It is a total transformation of a person's way of thinking, acting, and living. The Christian is not only in Christ, but Christ is in him or her through the softening power of the Holy Spirit. We can know that we are safe in Jesus when His PRINCIPLE of love becomes the guiding motivation in our lives. One of my favorite texts on the topic is John 13:35:

- "By this," said Jesus, "all men will know that you are my disciples, if you keep the Sabbath."
- "By this all men will know that you are my disciples, if you pay tithe."
- "By this all men will know that you are my disciples, if you have the proper diet."

I preached on that text (using the above distortions to illustrate my point) one time and had a brand-new Adventist come up to me. "My Bible," he exclaimed, "doesn't read that way in John 13! Where can I find that text?" He was after the ultimate Adventist proof text. In his exuberance, he had missed my emphasis on the actual reading: "By this all men will know that you are my disciples, if you have love for one another." How I treat my neighbor is the acid test of Christianity. Too long have Adventists applied John 14:15, "If you love me, you will keep my commandments," to the Ten Commandments. Read John 13, 14, and 15, and see what the context is. "I command you," Jesus says over and over in these chapters, "to love one another."

Out of that principle and only out of it comes a meaningful keeping of God's laws.

- Because I love my neighbor, I will not steal from him or her.
- Because I love my neighbor, I will not covet my neighbor's car, house, wife, or husband.
- Because I love my neighbor, I cannot use him or her as a sexual object for my own pleasure.
- Because I love my neighbor, I will want him or her to experience the joy of being safe in Jesus.
- Because I love my neighbor, I will want him or her to share the delights of the Sabbath.

Love to God and neighbor is the centerpiece of Christianity. It reflects the LAW that undergirds the laws. Neighbor love, as we will see in the rest of this book, stands at the center of sanctification, the emulation of Christ's character, judgment, and Christian perfection. "By this," said Jesus, "all men will know that you are my disciples, if you have love for one another."

Points to ponder

1. Last week you spoke to the local youth group on the major characteristics of SIN. You did such a good job that you have been invited to return and make a similar 20-minute presentation on LAW. List in full sentences the 4 or 5 major points of your outline.
2. Chapters 1 and 2 have argued that SIN and LAW are both love. How can they be the same thing? If they are both love, how can they be differentiated?
3. Is it presumptuous to say that the Ten Commandments are not universal or eternal? What Bible grounds can be given for such a claim?
4. What is the major problem with negative religion?
5. What is the purpose of the law? What limitations does the law have?
6. Explain how a person can keep the law of God and still be "meaner than the devil."
7. Why is it that Christians of necessity must keep God's law?

Notes

1. Ellen G. White to Willie and Mary White, March 13, 1890. Published in *The Ellen G. White 1888 Materials* (Washington, DC: Ellen G. White Estate, 1987), 632. For more on the "spirit of Minneapolis," see George R. Knight, *A User-Friendly Guide to the 1888 Message* (Hagerstown, MD: Review and Herald, 1998), 62-66.

2. Ellen G. White, *Spiritual Gifts* (Battle Creek, MI: Seventh-day Adventist Publishing Assn., 1864), III:295.

3. Ibid.

4. Ellen G. White, *Selected Messages* (Washington, DC: Review and Herald, 1958, 1980), I:220.

5. Ibid., 230.

6. Ellen G. White to Brothers and Sisters of the Iowa Conference, Nov. 6, 1901. Published in *The Ellen G. White 1888 Materials*, 1764.

7. William Barclay, *The Gospel of Matthew*, 2d ed. (Edinburgh: The Saint Andrew Press, 1958), II:57.

8. White, *Selected Messages*, I:320.

9. Ibid., 211.

10. A reference to the 1888 session of the General Conference of Seventh-day Adventists, held in Minneapolis, Minnesota. The doctrine of righteousness by faith was hotly debated at that meeting. See also note 1 above.

SANCTIFY: set apart as or declare holy; consecrate. make legitimate or binding by religious sanction.

CHAPTER THREE

JUSTIFY: show or prove to be right or reasonable.

RIGHTEOUS: (a person of conduct) morally right or justifiable; virtuous.

Justification the Work of a Lifetime
Sanctification the Work of a Moment

Now I am well aware of the fact that my title reverses the usual approach to the subject of justification and sanctification. But that doesn't mean that I'm wrong. When I preached the topics in this book at the annual meeting of the General Conference, some of the "brethren" accused me of not believing my sermon titles. I believe all of them.

This chapter will examine more closely the process of salvation as it affects our daily lives. What actually happens to us in the process of salvation? What does it mean to be justified and sanctified? And, beyond that, how meaningful are those terms when we speak of being saved?

While my topic may sound rather calm and pedestrian, it has been a primary battlefront down through church history. Dutch Calvinist G. C. Berkouwer makes that point when he writes, "In this controversy one accuses the other of allowing justification to be assimilated by sanctification, only to be told that he, on the other hand, through his preoccupation with justification, crowds out sanctification."[1] The battle over the relative importance of those two topics has waged in the Christian church for two millennia and is far from being settled. And Seventh-day Adventists are not a whit behind the most energetic in fighting this battle. This topic is at the forefront of the tension in the Seventh-day Adventist Church today. Dissension over this topic is leading the denomination's factions in different directions.

I will have more to say about the relationship between justification and sanctification later, but at this point I will give you a little preview of my conclusions by saying that from the New Testament perspective, both extremes on the relative importance of justification and sanctification are wrong. The major New Testament characterization of a person's being saved is much broader than either justification or sanctification. Of course, if I were the devil, I would be delighted if I could get Christians into a major battle over the relative importance of the two experiences. After all, my main object would be to make sure that people don't have them.

What happens when you come to Jesus?

We will now examine the categories themselves. What do I mean when I say that justification is the work of a lifetime? I do not mean that initial justification is not instantaneous. Ellen White was correct when she said that justification is the work of a moment. Justification is God's legal declaration that those who have accepted the sacrifice of Christ as their substitute are no longer under the condemnation of the broken law. Justification is a legal declaration, and it is totally by grace. That is, justification is 100 percent undeserved. Sinners—that means you and me—are rebels against God and deserve nothing, according to Romans 6:23, but eternal death. The New Testament is clear that there is nothing that sinners can do of themselves to become worthy of forgiveness. The broken law can only condemn. It has no provision in itself for forgiveness. But beyond condemning, the law points sinners to the solution. It points us to Jesus Christ and His blood for forgiveness and cleansing.

People are totally justified by grace, defined as God's unmerited favor. As such, it is impossible to overestimate the ir of justification. Without it, a person is not merely partial totally lost. Each person, according to Paul, has the po accepting God's justifying grace through a willingness t faith, which is also one of God's gifts. Paul sums the p nicely in Ephesians 2: "By grace you have been savec faith; and this is not your own doing, it is the gift of because of works, lest any man should boast" (Eph. 2:8 Moody, the famous nineteenth-century evangelist, was o to say, "If anybody ever gets to heaven because of anythi we will never hear the end of it." Because of the nature of sin and grace, none of those saved will ever have occasion to boast.

Faith is grabbing hold of grace, God's unmerited forgiveness in Christ. Faith is grabbing hold of what we don't deserve. The result is instantaneous. We are no longer under condemnation but are counted as righteous in the books of heaven. But—and this is my major point in saying that justification is the work of a lifetime—instantaneous or initial justification is not all there is to the topic. Initial justification is necessary and important, but the problem is that Christians continue to sin. They therefore stand in need of continuous justification.

Hans LaRondelle correctly suggests that we are in need of *"daily justification"* by faith in Christ, whether we have consciously transgressed or unknowingly erred."[2] Daily justification is closely tied to Christ's ministry on our behalf in the heavenly sanctuary. In Hebrews we read: "He always lives to make intercession" for "those who draw near to God through him" (Heb. 7:25). In Romans it is Christ "who is at the right hand of God,...[and] intercedes for us" (Rom. 8:34). And John writes, "If anyone does sin, we have an advocate with the Father, Jesus Christ the righteous" (1 John 2:1).

Some scholars prefer to think of ongoing justification as "continuing forgiveness," since their standing with God was corrected at the time of their conversion and initial justification. But in essence, the difference is largely semantic. Day by day, Christ continues to mediate for His earthly brothers and sisters and to declare them righteous before the heavenly mercy seat.

That brings us to sanctification as the work of a moment. In order to understand sanctification as the work of a moment, we need to look at what takes place when a person is initially justified. What happens when you come to Jesus?

The Bible links several events to initial justification. One is self-crucifixion or death to the old way of life. Crucifixion is a brutal term that implies the death of self-centered living—living that has self-love or SIN at its very core. Jesus told His disciples, "'If any man would come after me, let him deny himself and take up his cross and follow me. For whoever would save his life will lose it, and whoever loses his life for my sake will find it'" (Matt. 16:24, 25).

Now the cross is an instrument of death. It is not some thing or some person we have to put up with, such as an unfaithful wife or a nagging husband. The cross is an instrument of death. Dietrich Bonhoeffer says it nicely when he claims that "when Christ calls a man, he bids him come and die."[3]

The crucifixion of the self takes place when we come to God in faith, ask for forgiving and justifying grace, and put God back at the center of our lives in place of our own self. Crucifixion is death to self-centered living. It is death to the self-life. And that death takes place for us when we give our lives to God. Christ made provision for our personal crucifixion at the cross.

But at the very moment of self-crucifixion, the Bible tells us that something else happens to us. Justified Christians are also regenerated, born from above, resurrected to a new way of thinking and living based on God's LAW. What they once hated they now love and vice versa. Christians are described in the New Testament as new creatures, as new creations (2 Cor. 5:17). They walk in newness of life. Paul describes this process as a transformation of the mind (Rom. 12:2). The Greek word that he uses for

44

transformation is related to our English word "metamorphosis." If you are familiar at all with biology, you know that this is the same word biologists use to describe the process by which an ugly sluglike caterpillar becomes a beautiful butterfly with wings. Thus, a creature that could only crawl comes to fly through the miracle of metamorphosis. Metamorphosis denotes a change so radical, so complete, that unless people knew better, they wouldn't even recognize it as the same life.

So it is with Christian living. The Christian life is founded upon the crucifixion of the self-centered life principle of SIN and the resurrection to a new life based upon the other-centered LAW of love.

A third event pictured as taking place at the time of initial justification is repentance. Repentance can be viewed as the negative aspect of coming to Christ. If faith is seen as a turning to Christ, then repentance is a simultaneous turning away from SIN. As people turn to God in faith, they are at the same time repenting or turning away from their old life of self-centeredness. Another word for the same experience is conversion.

A fourth event that takes place simultaneously with initial justification is adoption—adoption into the family of God. For too long people have claimed that every human being is a child of God. That is not the teaching of the Bible. The Bible teaches that only those who enter into a covenant relationship with God are His children. We become children when we accept the Fatherhood and the Lordship of God. John writes: "To all who received him, who believed in his name, he gave power to become children of God; who were born, not of blood nor of the will of the flesh nor of the will of man, but of God" (John 1:12, 13). At the very moment a person accepts Jesus, he or she is adopted into the covenant family. These new Christians are reconciled not only to God but to His will and ways. It is in the adoption that we have our assurance of salvation. In the adoption we are safe in Jesus.

Christians are now a part of God's great covenant family and will remain so unless they subsequently choose to live a life characterized by rebellion against God. That is, they remain in God's family unless they choose SIN with a capital S and a capital I and a capital N—unless they choose SIN as a principle in their lives. God does not bounce us in and out of salvation, in and out of His family, because we have momentary or accidental or inadvertent sins. No! We are covered by the covenant blessings. We are in the family. We have a mediator above to handle those sins that are not rebellious SIN. The book of 1 John talks about sins that are unto death and sins not unto death. We will examine that topic in our fifth chapter.

My main point at the present time is that all those who choose to remain in God's great covenant family, in place of living a life of rebellion, have the assurance of their present salvation. They are safe in Jesus.

A deeper view of sanctification

Now beyond self-crucifixion, new birth, repentance, and adoption, there is at least one other thing that takes place at the moment of initial justification: sanctification, or what might be called "initial" sanctification. As such, sanctification is the work of a moment. That becomes clear when we realize that the very meaning of sanctification is "to be set apart for holy use." Thus the tabernacle in the wilderness, along with the priests and the furniture, were sanctified. They were set apart for holy use. They were consecrated to God. Likewise, in the New Testament a saint is one who is sanctified, one who is set apart for holy use, one who is consecrated to God. Thus Paul could claim that even the members of the rather disgusting Corinthian church were saints.

I still remember how confused I became the first time I tried to preach from the Bible on the difference between justification and sanctification. It was at a prayer meeting in the San Francisco Central Church. I came to the topic with the help of

Cruden's Concordance, but with the presupposition that sanctification was the work of a lifetime. I was thrown off track when I read such texts as Acts 26:18, 1 Corinthians 1:2, and Hebrews 10:10, which talk about sanctification as an accomplished fact, a past event in the lives of Christians. We "have been sanctified," we read in the book of Hebrews and other places. I was taken aback when I realized that the Bible often treated sanctification as an instantaneous past event. Only later was I able to see that our glib Adventist formulations failed to do complete justice to the Bible concept of sanctification. Only later did I realize that to account for all the facts, I needed to treat sanctification as at least a three-fold process.

First, when we come to Christ and are justified, we are also sanctified. That is, when we become Christians, not only do we receive instantaneous forgiveness and justification, but we become consecrated to God and are set aside for holy use. We become part of a holy people and a royal priesthood.

Unfortunately, getting instantaneously set apart for holy use does not make us instantaneously holy or totally sanctified. You may have discovered that. We still live in the same bodies and still have the old habit patterns—habit patterns that have been built up over an entire lifetime. We have been born again and set aside for holy use, but we are not mature (the word "mature" also is the biblical word for "perfect") in holiness.

I remember a few years back when I was teaching a philosophy course at Andrews University. That quarter I had an Arabian student sent by his government to study for a doctoral degree in educational administration. After I taught the place of religion in the scheme of things, my Islamic student came to my office and said, "I want to buy a copy of the Bible." He then asked, "Will you come to the bookstore and help me pick out a Bible?" Needless to say, we were soon off to make an important purchase.

About three weeks later, he returned to my office and said, "The strangest thing happened to me last Sunday. I went to a

Christian church for the first time. It was a Baptist church, and they did this strange thing. They dunked this man underwater, and when he came up they said he was a 'new creature.'" My friend then noted that the baptized man was not a "new creature" but the same man. He wanted to know the meaning of what he had witnessed. Of course, that was the beginning of an interesting Bible study that began that very moment. My point is that just because we are born again and baptized does not mean we are totally different or mature in Christ.

That brings us to the second level of sanctification. If "initial" sanctification sets us apart for holy use, then "progressive" sanctification is what the Bible writers refer to as "growth in grace." While initial sanctification is instantaneous, progressive sanctification is the work of a lifetime.

The third level of sanctification might be thought of as "final" sanctification or glorification. That, of course, takes place at the second coming of Christ, when Christians are "changed in a moment...at the last trumpet" (1 Cor. 15:51, 52).

What it means to grow in grace

Meanwhile, as I grew in understanding, I came to several other conclusions regarding sanctification. First—and I can't make this point strongly enough—we need to move beyond what I call "clothesline" sanctification. Too often, we have viewed sanctification as following a list of dos and don'ts. Thus for some Christians the essence of sanctified living is a matter of not eating between meals or not wearing certain types of garments. Christian living for such people degenerates into rigidly following a list of rules much like those kept by the Pharisees of old.

Closely related to the list approach is another favorite of the Pharisees—looking at the sanctified life in the negative. That is, people become "holy" by what they avoid. For too many people, Christian living consists in seeking "to be good by not being bad."

At the heart of all false avenues to sanctified living is a trivialization of righteousness through a breaking up of the righteous life into manageable blocks of behavior. Such an approach is directly related to the atomization of SIN and LAW we discussed earlier. It lends itself nicely to "clothesline preaching" and making such items as dietary reform and a person's outward dress the things to focus on in discussions of living the Christian life. That type of "sanctification" has an excellent historic pedigree. It was at the center of Pharisaic Judaism.

The "benefit" in the trivialization of sanctification and negative approaches to the topic is that they lower the standard to the place where it is conceivably possible to perfectly keep the various laws, rules, and regulations. Jesus, however, did a "hatchet job" on trivialization in the Sermon on the Mount, where He highlighted the depth and unity of the LAW by relating it to the LAW's underlying principle. When He told His listeners that their righteousness must exceed that of the scribes and Pharisees, He was moving them to a higher standard than that provided for by the atomization of righteousness and a list of dos and don'ts. Christianity represents salvation from SIN with a capital S, not merely salvation from sins. According to the Bible, the essence of sanctification is a total transformation of heart leading to a change of life that includes the way we treat and view ourselves, our neighbors, and God. <u>Progressive sanctification is the process by which selfish and self-centered people are transformed into lovers of God and other people.</u>

Sanctification is nothing less than the process by which Christians become progressively more loving. Let me say that again. *<u>Sanctification is the process by which Christians become progressively more loving</u>*. That is what sanctification is all about. Those lifestyle issues that we have confused with sanctification are means to an end, not ends in themselves.

Health reform, for example, is an aid to sanctification. After all, it has been discovered by those who have to live with me that

I am not a very loving person when I'm sick. In fact, I'm often grouchy, self-centered, and sometimes mean when I don't feel well. God wants me to be happy and loving. He wants me, therefore, to be healthy. Health reform is a means to an end rather than an end in itself. The good lifestyle issues that we hold so dear as a church are means to a good end. The tragedy is that too often we have made them into ends in themselves and have in the process confused character with lifestyle. We have confounded sanctification with a list of dos and don'ts. There is a relationship between the two but not an equation.

A second thing we need to examine in relationship to sanctification is the fact that the New Testament is dead set against works—that is, certain types of works. The New Testament is especially set against three types of works: (1) works of the flesh (Rom. 8:3-10), which are the outworkings of the sinful human nature; (2) works of law (Rom. 3:28; Gal. 2:16; Eph. 2:9), which are carried out in the hope of gaining salvation; and (3) dead works (Heb. 6:1), which are the activities of individuals out of relationship to God and thus devoid of the power of grace.

Works of faith

But the New Testament is not against all works. Over against those less-than-helpful works are works of faith. There is a vast difference between works of faith in the New Testament and other types of works.

Paul speaks approvingly of "faith working through love" (Gal. 5:6). He commends the Thessalonians' "work of faith and labor of love" (1 Thess. 1:3). And part of his task was to call the Gentiles to "the obedience of faith" (Rom. 1:5; 16:26).

Jesus also made it plain that there were "good" works and "bad" works. For example, in Matthew 7 He tells of rejecting some in the final judgment who had done "many mighty works" in His name. But in the same passage He also says that "he who does the will of my Father" will be in the kingdom (verses 21, 22). Paul clarifies the distinction between "good" and "bad" works when he says, "Whatever does not proceed from faith is sin" (Rom. 14:23).

A legal work is one done out of our own resources in an attempt to gain favor or salvation from God. On the other hand, works of faith flow out of a saving relationship with Jesus, are energized by the power of the Holy Spirit, and are shaped and softened by the love of the Father.

An understanding of the correct relationship between works and justification (being put right with God), the new birth, and initial sanctification is crucial. A saved person does not work to get saved any more than a tree produces fruit to prove that it is alive. A tree produces fruit because it is alive. A saved person produces good works because he or she is alive in Christ.

Martin Luther had it right when he wrote in his preface to the book of Romans that "it is a living, busy, active, mighty thing, this faith; and so it is impossible for it not to do good works incessantly.... It is impossible to separate works from faith, quite as impossible as to separate heat and light [from] fires."[4]

A third point that we need to understand in relationship to progressive sanctification is the place of human effort. Some Christian writers seem to imply that "Jesus does it all." I used to believe that Jesus did it all, but soon discovered that when I lay in bed in the morning nothing got done. I used to teach that the sum total of human works was striving to stay surrendered. While I still believe that there is much truth in that line of thought, I have come to the conclusion that it fails to do justice to either the richness of the biblical language on the topic or to daily experience. The Bible is laced with words and stories that imply human effort.

The New Testament is full of action words. The Bible picture is not one of the saints being carried to heaven on beds of ease. But neither does the Bible teach the efficacy of human effort separated from God's empowerment. "Apart from me," Christ said, "you can do nothing" (John 15:5). The picture is rather one of cooperation between God and human beings. Thus Paul can write, "I also labour, striving according to his working, which worketh in me mightily" (Col. 1:29, KJV), and "I can do all things in him who strengthens me" (Phil. 4:13).

In a similar manner, when the children of Israel were ready to cross the Red Sea, Moses told them, "'Stand firm, and see the salvation of the Lord, which he will work for you today.... The Lord will fight for you, and you have only to be still.'" OK, you may be thinking, there it is—God does it all. But the next verse says that God commanded the people to "'go forward'" (Exod. 14:13-15). God opened the way, but He didn't carry the people. They crossed the dry seabed through their own effort.

Thus there is both a passive and an active element in our walk with God. First comes surrender, then comes spirit-empowered action that requires human effort and cooperation. Perhaps the clearest text on the interaction of God's working and human effort is Paul's admonition to the Philippians: "Work out your own salvation with fear and trembling; for God is at work in you, both to will and to work for his good pleasure" (Phil. 2:12, 13). In summary, human effort is important and needed. While effort does not lead to salvation, it certainly flows from it.

The unity of salvation

Perhaps the most important understanding (and one that is at the heart of this book) that we can gain is that it is meaningless—absolutely meaningless—to speak of justification in the Christian experience without at the same time talking about sanctification. Likewise, it is of no use to consider sanctification in the Christian experience without thinking about justification. The two go hand in hand.

- Both are the work of the moment.
- Both are the work of a lifetime.
- Both are by God's grace.

Too often, we have tried to put distance between the aspects of God's great act of salvation.

James Denny, a major theologian in the first part of the twentieth century, was speaking to that point when he wrote: "It has sometimes [been] forgotten that the great matter is not the distinction of justification and sanctification, but their connection, and that justification or reconciliation is a delusion unless the life of the reconciled and justified is inevitably and naturally a holy life." These two aspects of salvation are "the indivisible and all-inclusive response of the soul to Christ."[5] The great Reformers of the sixteenth century saw this truth clearly. Calvin could therefore write that "Christ justifies no one whom he does not at the same time sanctify.... You cannot possess him [Christ] without being made partaker in his sanctification, because he cannot be divided."[6]

On the other hand, please recognize that for purposes of abstract theoretical discussion, justification and sanctification can be separated, but not in life. Paul does discuss them sequentially in the book of Romans. In the early chapters he discusses justification, while the later chapters deal with sanctification. Such divided discussion can take place in the abstract, but the very moment a person accepts Jesus in experience, the justified individual is also sanctified. It is nonbiblical to speak of a person as only being justified or only being sanctified. One who is justified is also sanctified, and the one who is truly sanctified is also justified.

The Bible is not nearly as concerned with discussing the fine lines of distinction between justification and sanctification as it is in speaking to meaningful Christianity. The Bible is not a systematic theology. The New Testament does not argue whether sanctification is more important than justification or whether one comes before the other. The real issue, from the perspective of the New Testament, is whether a person is in a faith relationship with Jesus Christ. That is the issue—the only issue. SIN is breaking a relationship with God, while FAITH is entering into and maintaining a relationship with Him. To have FAITH is to be safe in Jesus.

To make decisions (knowing) having FAITH that God will take care of you and the consequences.

53

Paul is especially clear that a person is either "in Adam" or "in Christ" (1 Cor. 15:22; Rom. 5:12-21). Those who are "in Christ" are justified, sanctified, and are being progressively sanctified and perfected. "In Christ" is a key concept in Paul. That phrase (or one of its equivalents) occurs 164 times in Paul's letters—eleven times in one of the great opening sentences of the book of Ephesians.

The Judge is on your side

The "in Christ" perspective brings us to the topic of judgment. There is an important question that naturally arises once people accept the Bible's teaching that God's people have already been saved and have "eternal life" (John 3:36; 5:24). If, the question runs, we have already been saved in Christ, if we are safe in Him, why does God need a final judgment?

Now judgment has not always been a popular subject. That distaste is not too difficult to understand in nonbelievers, but for a Christian to get upset or fearful over the topic shows a lack of understanding concerning the character of God and the very nature of His judgment.

The biblical Judge is, after all, not against us.

- The Judge sent the Saviour.
- The Judge made the propitiation possible.
- The Judge loved us so much that He gave His only Son.

It is crucial to understand that God as our Judge is on our side. He is not against us or even neutral. He sent His Son because He loves us and wants to save as many people as possible. And He will save all those who will be happy in His kingdom.[7] Thus judgment is not a fearful thing to a Christian.

God's purpose in the judgment is the vindication of believers through confirmation that they are "in Christ." There can be, penned Paul, "no condemnation for those who are in Christ Jesus" (Rom. 8:1). "If God is for us, who is against us?... It is God who justifies [counts righteous]; who is to condemn?" Christ "is at the right hand of God" to intercede "for us." Nothing can separate those "in Christ" from the love of God (Rom. 8:31-39). The Christian, therefore, can look forward to the final acts of judgment with peace and joy. Christians already have assurance because they are safe in Jesus. "He who believes in the Son," John wrote, "has eternal life; he who does not obey the Son shall not see life" (John 3:36).

The judgment is God saying Yes to us because we have said Yes to Christ. The judgment is God saying, "Yes, this person has accepted My Son into his or her heart and has, as a result, internalized the great principle of love." Those who have the love of God in their hearts will be saved. Thus the judgment, in one sense, is a vindication of the saints.

- The good news is that God the Judge is for us.
- The good news is that all who are in Christ have already been saved and will be both vindicated and more fully saved at the end of all things.
- The good news is that all who love and maintain a faith relationship with Jesus Christ already have assurance of salvation.
- The good news is that Christians are safe in Jesus.

Points to ponder
1. Congratulations! During the past two weeks you made presentations to the local youth group on the characteristics of SIN and LAW. People are excited about what you had to say. As a result, they are clamoring for you to speak again—this time for 20 minutes on what happens to a person when he or she comes to Jesus. List and describe in a sentence or two the major points of your outline.
2. "Justification" is a meaningless word to many people—some kind of theological mumbo jumbo. Define the word in concrete language. Explain how justification can be both the work of a moment and the work of a lifetime.

3. "Sanctification" is another important word that is often mis-understood. What is the most basic one-sentence definition of sanctification? Briefly describe the three levels of sancti-fication. What is the essence of "progressive sanctification"?

4. If "works" don't save us, what place do they have in the Christian life? How do they relate to salvation? What is the difference between "good" works and "bad" works?

5. What is the difference between passive and active right-eousness?

6. In what sense is the judgment good news?

Notes

1. G. C. Berkouwer, *Faith and Sanctification*, John Vriend, trans. (Grand Rapids, MI: Eerdmans, 1952), 9.

2. Hans K. LaRondelle, *Christ Our Salvation: What God Does for Us and in Us* (Mountain View, CA: Pacific Press, 1980), 45.

3. Dietrich Bonhoeffer, *The Cost of Discipleship*, rev. ed. (New York: Collier, 1963), 99.

4. Martin Luther, *Commentary on Romans*, trans. J. T. Mueller (Grand Rapids, MI: Kregel, 1976), xvii.

5. James Denney, *The Christian Doctrine of Reconciliation* (London: James Clarke, 1959), 297, 300.

6. John Calvin, *Institutes of the Christian Religion*, Ford Lewis Battles, trans. (Philadelphia: Westminster, 1960), I: 798 (3.16.1).

7. Those who will be happy in God's kingdom, of course, are those who are willing to live in harmony with God's great LAW of love, which will affect every part of their lives. For more on this topic, see George R. Knight, *The Pharisee's Guide to Perfect Holiness: A Study of Sin and Salvation* (Boise, ID: Pacific Press, 1992), 123-126; George R. Knight, *My Gripe with God: A Study in Divine Justice and the Problem of the Cross* (Washington, DC: Review and Herald, 1990), 98, 99, 113-118.

CHAPTER FOUR

Temptation is not TEMPTATION

As you looked at the title of this chapter, you recognized that one use of temptation has capital letters all the way through, while the other one does not. And by this time you have probably discovered my shorthand system. The capitalization has a crucial message in itself. What I'm seeking to convey is the important difference between TEMPTATION with a capital T, a capital E, and so on, as opposed to temptations. There is a central TEMPTATION that stands at the very core of the Christian life. That TEMPTATION is the source of all individual or itemized temptations. As a result,

TEMPTATION → temptations

As you might have already guessed, the central TEMPTA-TION is related to the central SIN, which spawns all other sins. It is also related to the central principle of love in the LAW, which gives birth to all derivative laws, and it is related to the central RIGHTEOUSNESS of being in Christ, which leads to all righteous acts.

Avoiding the cross: the essence of TEMPTATION

TEMPTATION is not temptation. To hear some people talk, one would guess that TEMPTATION has to do with whether one should steal a car, go to a movie, eat too much sugar, or play golf too often. Those things may be temptations, but they are not TEMPTATION.

Christ's life illustrates the nature of TEMPTATION with a capital T, the parent of all temptations. That TEMPTATION was for Jesus to do His own thing, to live His own life, to avoid His cross. A key to understanding Christ's TEMPTATION is Philippians 2:5-8: "Have this mind among yourselves," Paul wrote to the believers, "which is yours in Christ Jesus, who, though he was in the form of God, did not count equality with God a thing to be grasped, but emptied himself, taking the form of a servant, being born in the likeness of men. And being found in human form he humbled himself and became obedient unto death, even death on a cross."

Note that Christ, the God-man, "emptied himself" of something when He became a human being. While the apostle does not define the full meaning of those words, it seems clear from a study of the rest of the New Testament that part of what Jesus did in becoming human was to strip Himself voluntarily—and "voluntarily" is the key word—of the insignia and prerogatives of Deity. Thus Paul seems to be saying in part that Christ voluntarily gave up the independent use of His divine attributes and submitted to all the conditions of human life.

In other words, Jesus remained God but voluntarily chose not to use His divine powers on His own behalf. Like other people, He remained dependent upon the Father and the Holy Spirit's power during His earthly existence. Yet He met Satan's challenge that obedience to the law was impossible. In His perfect life of obedience, Jesus overcame where Adam failed, but He did so as a human being rather than as God. In His reliance upon His Father and the power of the Spirit for daily strength, He had the same help that we may have in our daily lives.

The crucial point is that because Jesus had voluntarily emptied Himself, He could resume divine power at any moment He chose to do so. It was a matter of the will. Unlike other human beings, Jesus could have used His awesome powers as God at any split second. To do so, however, would have defeated the plan of salvation in which He came to disprove Satan's claim that God's law could not be kept by human beings.

It is at the point of Christ's voluntary self-emptying that we find the focus and the strength of His temptations throughout His life. If the enemy had been able to get Jesus to "unempty" Himself even one time and get Him to use His "hidden" power in anger or on His own behalf, the war would have been over.

The item to note is that Jesus was not only tempted "in every respect...as we are" (Heb. 4:15), but that He was tempted far beyond the point where ordinary human beings can ever possibly be tempted, since Jesus actually had the power of God "in" His fingertips rather than "at" His fingertips. The great struggle of Christ was to stay emptied. That is the significance of the temptation to "command" stones to become loaves of bread (Matt. 4:3).

Now I want you to know that that temptation is no temptation to me at all, because I can't do it. I could go out in the church parking lot and command all day. But two years from now, I would still be out there without a single loaf to show for my effort. On the other hand, Jesus could do it. As the agent of creation of all that exists, He had the ability to make bread out of nothing.

Jesus had been without food for more than a month when the temptation concerning the bread came to Him. Certainly it must have been an attractive suggestion, but we miss the point if we see it merely as a temptation to satisfy His appetite. That was a temptation with a small t, not THE TEMPTATION with a capital T. The real TEMPTATION was to reverse the self-emptying of Philippians 2 by using His divine power to satisfy His personal needs. That, of course, would have meant that He was not facing the world like other people. Underlying the TEMPTATION was the subtle insinuation that "if" He were truly God He could use His special powers for Himself instead of relying on the Father.

Some circles in Adventism engage in a great deal of discussion regarding what it meant for Jesus to be tempted "in every respect...as we are, yet [be] without sin" (Heb. 4:15). Too often, we have fought the issue as if it depended upon some definition of the human nature of Christ. But I would like to submit that from a simple reading of the Bible we find that Jesus, irrespective of the constitution of His human nature, was tempted far beyond the point that any other person can ever be tempted. Most of His temptations are not even temptations to me, because I lack the ability to respond to them successfully.

All Christ's temptations were centered on having Him give up His dependency on the Father—to take control of His own life by becoming "unemptied."

Closely related to that issue was the enticement to follow His own will rather than following the will of the Father, especially as God's will led to humbling Himself and becoming "obedient unto death, even death on a cross" (Phil. 2:8). Christ's special TEMPTATION throughout His life was to avoid death on the cross. That was the essential power of the bread temptation in the wilderness. Two things were in full supply in Palestine: rocks and hungry people. To make bread from rocks would be an easier, more pleasant, and more immediate route to the kingdom than a cross. After all, look what happened in John 6 when Jesus, for the sake of others, did provide bread from heaven when He fed the five thousand. They said, "Ha, this is another Moses, another manna provider. Let's make Him king." And even the disciples got carried away with that idea (see John 6:14, 15, 30, 31; Matt. 14:22). That was TEMPTATION to Jesus, to achieve the kingdom by some method other than the cross.

The TEMPTATION to avoid the cross also explains the forcefulness of Christ's rejection of Peter's suggestion that Jesus did not need to "suffer many things from the elders and chief priests and scribes, and be killed." "'Get behind me, Satan!'" was Christ's unparalleled rebuke of His disciple (Matt. 16:21, 23).

The cross does not hold much meaning for me in the twentieth century. I've never seen a crucifixion. Jesus had. When He saw a knot of Roman soldiers escorting a man dragging a cross through the streets, He knew it was a one-way trip. And, like any normal human being, He had no desire to exit the world by the way of the excruciating death of the cross. It would have been much easier to become the political messiah that the Jews (including the disciples) desired. Beyond that, Jesus had no wish to bear the judgment of the world by becoming "sin" for all humanity in the great sacrifice on Calvary (2 Cor. 5:21). The thought of separation from God while bearing the sins of the world on the cross was abhorrent to Him.

The TEMPTATION to do His own will by avoiding the cross came to a head in Gethsemane as He came face to face with the full meaning of the cross. At that time the Bible tells us that Jesus was "greatly distressed and troubled" and asked that "if it were possible, the hour might pass from him" (Mark 14:33, 35).

Fighting the TEMPTATION to do His own will and back off from the cross, Jesus underwent duress that we can understand only faintly. In great agony and dread, Jesus finally made His decision. "'My Father,'" He repeatedly prayed, "'if this cannot pass unless I drink it, thy will be done'" (Matt. 26:42).

The TEMPTATION to come down from the cross

On the cross itself, Jesus faced the combined force of the two aspects of His TEMPTATION: to do His own will by coming down from the cross and to use His power for His personal benefit.

A major difference between Jesus' crucifixion and every other Roman crucifixion was that He did not have to stay on the cross. He could have come down. He was not a helpless victim. As the Man who was God, He could have "unemptied" Himself and ended the ordeal.

Jesus, however, had chosen to die on the cross. It was a matter of the will. His crucifixion was a voluntary act of obedience to God's will. "'I lay down my life.... No one takes it from me, but I lay it down of my own accord.'" "'The good shepherd lays down his life for the sheep'" (John 10:17, 18, 11). Thus Christ could have come down from the cross, but He would not come down.

All through Jesus' life, Satan tempted Him away from the cross, and he carried forth that same program during the crucifixion itself as he tempted Jesus to "unempty" Himself and do His own will. This time the tempter used the very persons whom Christ was dying for. Passersby derided Him, crying out that He had made great statements about what He could do. If you are who you claim to be, they challenged, "save yourself, and come down from the cross!" The chief priests and scribes also got into the act, mocking Him to one another and saying, "'He saved others; he cannot save himself. Let the Christ, the King of Israel, come down now from the cross, that we may see and believe.'" Meanwhile, some of the Roman guard "also mocked him" (Mark 15:30-32; Luke 23:36).

How would you have responded to such challenges and treatment if you were hanging naked on the cross and had access to such power? I'll tell you what I think I would have done to such ungrateful people. I would have gotten off my cross and given them exactly what they deserved. I would have demonstrated precisely who I was. I would have called down a little fire from heaven and zapped them with a slow sizzle. Of course, with a flick of my finger, I could have provided them with a localized nuclear holocaust. But in my human nature I would have opted for the slow sizzle because I would want these people to have time to think about my dignity and whom they had insulted. I would have proved exactly who I was. Such ungratefuls would certainly be sorry that they had exhausted my patience, especially when I was trying so hard to do them a favor.

Fortunately for the universe, Christ did not fall for Satan's ploy. He resisted the TEMPTATION to get off the cross, to put His own will and authority at the center of His life, and therefore to do "His own thing." Thus He overcame where Adam failed. Not only did His death cancel the penalty for sin, but His life provided an example for Christians to emulate. The cry "'It is finished'" (John 19:30) in part meant that He had lived a life of surrendered obedience, proving once for all to the universe that it could be done. Because of His love for us, He stayed on His cross to the end and thus could utter the words "'It is finished'" as a shout of victory.

Jesus' TEMPTATION is your TEMPTATION

The cross stands just as much at the center of TEMPTATION in my life and in your life as it did in Christ's. Remember that Adam and Eve fell when they rebelled against God and thus put their wills at the center of their lives and put their own selves in the commanding position that belonged to God. They fell when they redirected their love from God to themselves. SIN is a rebellious, broken relationship with God that puts my self and my will on the throne of my life. Out of that broken relationship flows a series of sinful actions (sins).

The New Testament imperative is the crucifixion of self-centeredness for every individual disciple of Christ, coupled with a new life to be lived in resurrection power (Rom. 6:1-11). "'If any man would come after me,'" said Jesus, "'let him deny himself and take up his cross and follow me'" (Matt. 16:24). "I have been crucified with Christ," claimed Paul; "it is no longer I who live, but Christ who lives in me; and the life I now live in the flesh I live by faith in the Son of God, who loved me and gave himself for me" (Gal. 2:20). The crucifixion of the self-centered, willful self stands at the very heart of Christianity.

The imitation of Christ is infinitely more than the development of a set of moral habits. It means much more than what I eat, wear, or watch. As the Pharisees of all ages have proved, a person can be morally upstanding yet still be self-centered, proud, and mean. A person can be moral without being crucified. A person can be moral without being safe in Jesus. Martin Luther discovered that. When Luther entered the monastery, writes Dietrich Bonhoeffer, "he had left everything behind except his pious self." But when he met Christ, "even that was taken from him."[1]

The gospel call is for crucifixion and transformation rather than a gradual improvement of the self-centered life (Rom. 12:1, 2). To pass from the self-centered spirit that is natural to humanity to the spirit of Christ is not a matter of gentle growth or natural evolution. Rather, claims H. H. Farmer, "it is an uprooting, rending, tearing, splitting and breaking, surgical-operation kind of thing." It is a crucifixion.[2]

The center of the struggle is the individual human will, what Ellen White calls "the governing power in the nature of man."[3] Thus she could write that "the warfare against self is the greatest battle that was ever fought. The yielding of self, surrendering all to the will of God, requires a struggle; but the soul must submit to God before it can be renewed in holiness."[4]

As James Denny put it: "Though sin may have a natural birth it does not die a natural death; in every case it has to be morally sentenced and put to death."[5] That sentencing is an act of the will under the impulse of the Holy Spirit.

As with Christ, the struggle to go to our cross will be the severest of our lives, because, as P. T. Forsyth points out, "our will is our dearest life, the thing we cling to most and give up last."[6] "God alone," penned Ellen White, "can give us the victory" in this struggle with our precious willful self. But He cannot and will not force our wills. "The stronghold of Satan" is only broken as the "will" is "placed on the side of God's will." But the strength for victory comes from God. "If you are 'willing to be made willing,' God will accomplish the work for you."[7]

Please note that Christians do not give up their wills. They do not become mindless putty in the hands of an omnipotent God. Rather, they give over their wills to the transforming power of God's Spirit. The will still remains the controlling power in Christians' lives, but the converted will is no longer contrary to God. Rather, it is in harmony with God and His principles. The rule of SIN as misdirected love is rooted out, and the great central principle of the LAW becomes a Christian's motivating guide. Christians do not become automatons in the hands of God, but responsible agents who share His viewpoint. Born-from-above Christians' hearts and minds will be so in harmony with God's will "that when obeying Him" they "shall be but carrying out" their "own impulses."[8]

Christ had His cross, and I have mine. You have yours. He died on His for our sins, in which He had no share; and we die on our cross to all pride and self-reliance, that we might partake of His life. At the cross of Christ, all intellectual and moral independence is finally broken, and we freely admit our dependence on God in every aspect of our lives. From the viewpoint of the cross, the words of Christ take on new meaning: "'Whoever would save his life will lose it'"; but "'whoever loses his life for my sake...will save it'" (Luke 9:24).

If coming to Jesus for justification and regeneration can be viewed as initial crucifixion, then the sanctified life should be seen as living the life of the cross. Thus Christ told His disciples to take up their crosses "daily" (Luke 9:23), and Paul asserted: "I die every day" (1 Cor. 15:31).

Just as TEMPTATION in Christ's life was (1) to depend on Himself and not go to the cross and (2) to come down from the cross, so it is with His followers. The TEMPTATION is always present:

- to come down from our crosses and give people exactly what they "deserve,"

- to "do our own thing,"
- to become the gods of our own lives,
- to make the Adam choice rather than the Christ choice.

TEMPTATION and your will

Like Jesus in His TEMPTATION, we also have free will and the power of choice. Just as Jesus could have chosen to frustrate the plan of salvation by not going to the cross, so can we. Likewise, just as Jesus could have gotten down from His cross to give people what they deserved, so can we.

Our great TEMPTATION is not to eat this item or to do that thing but to break our relationship with the Father, to step outside the FAITH relationship and to enter the SIN relationship of rebellion. Thus TEMPTATION is to choose to step outside the protective love of God. TEMPTATION is to choose to no longer abide in Jesus.

In a similar vein, to opt for TEMPTATION is to no longer be safe from both the condemnation and the power of sin. Let me illustrate.

I have known for years that I cannot sincerely pray and commit a deliberate act of sin at the same moment. I have experimented. Temptation can become sin at the point that I become conscious of the temptation as a temptation. At that very point, I can choose to do one of two things. I can reject the temptation through God's power, or I can choose to dwell on the temptation and cherish it a bit. In other words, I can ask God into my life to help me overcome, or I can tell Him to leave me alone for a while so that I can enjoy my private sin. I comfort myself that I will pray about it later. Too often, we are like Augustine, who, in suffering with the major temptation of his life, prayed, "Make me chaste, Lord, but not quite yet."

The alternative is to come to God, saying, "Lord, I recognize this temptation for what it is, and I am going to pray right now." I have personally discovered that when I sincerely and persever-ingly pray for victory, I lose the desire for the sin. I believe that

that phenomenon is the power of God helping me overcome both TEMPTATION and SIN, as well as temptations and sins.

But sometimes I don't want the power or the victory. I want the sin. At that point, I fall for TEMPTATION in the same way that Eve did in Genesis 3. I have actively taken charge of my own life and sidelined God. To actively and consistently choose TEMP- TATION leads to a life of falling for temptations as I separate myself from God. But the basic human problem is not tempta- tions. The basic human problem is TEMPTATION—to avoid the cross, to avoid the Christ life, to avoid being safe in Jesus, to choose the life of self-willed rebellion over the life of faith.

It is important to realize that TEMPTATION, in terms of its conscious or deliberate intent, is closely related to biblical sin- lessness and perfection. That is the topic of the next chapter. We will close this chapter by summarizing the characteristics of the sinless life in light of the lessons from this chapter.

- The sinless life is the life of faith.
- The sinless life is the life safe in Jesus.
- The sinless life is the life that follows Christ to the cross.
- The sinless life is the life that stays with Christ on the cross.
- The sinless life is the life of not opting for TEMPTATION.

To follow the example of Christ means not only to go to the cross but to live the life of the cross. To follow the example of Christ is to avoid TEMPTATION. "Let this mind be in you," wrote the apostle, "which was also in Christ Jesus: Who, being in the form of God...made himself of no reputation, and took upon him the form of a servant, and...humbled himself, and became obedi- ent unto death, even the death of the cross" (Phil. 2:5-8, KJV).

Points to ponder
1. The high price of success is more work. Your first three presentations to the local youth group have been a smash- ing success. You may not believe this, but they want you to

make a presentation this week on the nature of temptation. Outline your four or five main points, using full sentences to make the substance of your points crystal clear.

2. Define TEMPTATION as opposed to temptations.

3. How is TEMPTATION related to SIN, LAW, and RIGHTEOUSNESS?

4. What were the two aspects of Christ's TEMPTATION? How do these two aspects relate to TEMPTATION in your individual life?

5. How does the will relate to the problem of temptation?

6. At what point does temptation become sin? What are some strategies you can utilize to avoid crossing that line?

Notes

1. Bonhoeffer, *Cost of Discipleship*, 51.

2. H. H. Farmer, quoted in F. W. Dillistone, *The Significance of the Cross* (Philadelphia: Westminster, 1944), 155.

3. White, *Steps to Christ*, 47.

4. Ibid., 43.

5. Denney, *Christian Doctrine of Reconciliation*, 198.

6. P. T. Forsyth, *The Cruciality of the Cross* (Wake Forest, NC: Chanticleer, 1983), 92.

7. White, *Mount of Blessing*, 142.

8. White, *Desire of Ages*, 668.

CHAPTER FIVE

Perfect but Not Yet PERFECT
Sinless but Not Yet SINLESS

"You...must be perfect, as your heavenly Father is perfect" (Matt. 5:48). In this text Jesus not only issues the command for perfection, but He sets up God as the standard for that perfection.

"Walk before me, and be thou perfect," God commanded Abraham (Gen. 17:1, KJV). The book of Hebrews tells us to "go on unto perfection" (Heb. 6:1, KJV), and Paul wrote to the Colossians that he desired to "present every man perfect in Christ Jesus" (Col. 1:28, KJV). Spiritual gifts were given "for the perfecting of the saints" (Eph. 4:12, KJV; see also vs. 13).

The only thing one can conclude from the Bible is that perfection must be possible, or its writers would not have urged it upon believers. Thus the issue is not whether perfection is possible, but what the Bible writers mean by perfection.

Helpful and not-so-helpful perspectives on perfection

Before examining the Bible to ascertain the meaning of the word "perfection," it will be helpful to look at several preliminary aspects of the topic. First, a lot of confusion can be avoided if we recognize that perfection has more than one meaning in a believer's life. Marvin Moore correctly notes that "in one sense, we are perfect in Jesus the moment we accept Him as our

Saviour, because His righteousness covers our sins." In addition, however, "character perfection continues during one's entire lifetime."[1] Thus there are biblical concepts of perfection related to both justification and progressive sanctification. A third biblical concept of perfection is related to glorification, when our physical natures are transformed at the second coming of Christ (1 Cor. 15:51-54).

It is crucial to note that perfection as it relates to justification is not what the Bible is talking about in such texts as Matthew 5:48, Hebrews 6:1, and Ephesians 4:12, 13 (all quoted above). Those texts are speaking of a dynamic process of character development in which people really do become more and more like their "heavenly Father."

Paul refers to the dynamic aspect of perfection when he suggests to the Corinthians that they "make [their] holiness perfect in the fear of God" (2 Cor. 7:1). Those dynamics are also in view when the author of Hebrews tells believers to "go on unto perfection" (Heb. 6:1, KJV) and when the Corinthians are told that they "are being changed into his likeness from one degree of glory to another" (2 Cor. 3:18; compare Gal. 4:19; 2 Pet. 3:18).

Perfection is too often thought of as a "fixed" and "static" standard, whereas the Christian ideal must be thought of in terms of endless enrichment. Perfection is a line rather than a point to be achieved. "The word *point*," notes Moore, "is too limiting. Perfection is more a state of being, more a relationship with Jesus, more a way of life, than it is a 'point' that one can measure to know when he has reached it."[2]

The dynamic "line" of character development is infinite. "Perfect Christians" always become more and more like God without ever becoming just like Him. Heaven will be a place of eternal spiritual growth. Yet we will never be absolutely perfect in the sense that God is perfect, even in the ceaseless ages of eternity. To be absolutely perfect, by definition, would be to be God.

It is unfortunate that unbiblical teachings related to perfection and sinlessness have repeatedly led to excesses and fanaticism down through history. Thus John Wesley, a man who spent his life teaching the possibility of perfection, referred to some perfectionists who "made the very name of Perfection stink in the nostrils."[3]

Perverted theories of perfection have led to several aberrations among Christians. One perversion of the doctrine surrenders the clear distinction between the believer's will and the will of the Holy Spirit. Thus because a person is "perfect" by definition, whatever he or she does is right and sanctified. Such people can do no wrong because they are perfect. That teaching in the 1840s led to "spiritual wifery" and other perversions among ex-Millerite Adventists and other Christians.[4]

A second misguided approach to perfection leads in a materialistic direction. Thus the 1890s saw some holiness and Adventist groups believing that even their gray hairs would be restored to their natural color when they got right with God. And such preachers as E. J. Waggoner of 1888 fame taught that one who truly had Christ's righteousness would never get sick.[5]

A third misdirection of perfectionism is a moralism that uplifts external conformity to law. In moralistic perfection, every human act becomes regulated by laws that become increasingly complex and cover every aspect of diet, recreation, dress, and so on. Holiness through celibacy, flagellation, vegetarianism and other dietary restrictions, and even self-castration have not been uncommon among believers holding to moralistic views of perfection among both Protestants and Roman Catholics. Desperately in earnest, people of this persuasion develop long lists of rules, and the more they read, the longer their lists become. Many Pharisees and monks belonged to this camp of perfectionism, and Adventists and other conservative Christians in the modern world have often joined in.

A fourth misunderstanding of New Testament perfection substitutes the legal perfection of justification for the progressive perfection of character development. We are perfect in Christ, the theory runs, and that is all that is required. This theory is based on the fiction that character can be transferred from one person to another. Thus Christ became our vicarious perfection. Such a belief leads to logical antinomianism (rejection of the moral law) in thought if not in practice. Seventh-day Adventists at times have been caught up in this unbiblical form of perfection—a teaching directly related to the theory that justification can be separated from sanctification (discussed in chapter 3).

Biblical perfection

One of the most serious problems among Christians with regard to perfection is that people bring their own definitions of perfection to the Bible rather than letting the Bible define perfection for them. That procedure usually leads people to view perfection in absolutist terms that may be in harmony with Greek philosophy but do not reflect the biblical use of the word.

The Bible knows nothing of the Greek absolutist definition of human perfection. It is high time that Adventists realize that the influence of Greek philosophy in Christian theology was much broader than the condition of people in death. Another part of that apostasy was the imposition of absolutist, static definitions of perfection over dynamic Hebrew and New Testament ideas. The ascetic life of the monk in the Middle Ages was one result of that verbal confusion. While most Adventists are not tempted to join a monastery, many have been led astray by the definition of perfection that underlies that medieval institution.

The importing of foreign meanings for perfection into the biblical text has played havoc with the concept and has hindered understanding. In seeking to determine the biblical meaning of perfection, we need to let the context of the passage using the word be the commentary on its meaning. Beyond that, we should seek to discover the biblical meaning of the words used to translate our English word perfection.

Of the Gospel writers, only Matthew uses the term "perfect," and he uses it only three times. The first two uses are in the frustrating saying of chapter 5:48: "You, therefore, must be perfect, as your heavenly Father is perfect." While that text has sent people off on frenzied tangents of extremism in lifestyle and monastic discipline in the hope that separation from the world and sinners might enable them to be as perfect as God, the context suggests just the opposite course of action.

Being perfect as the Father is perfect, according to verses 43 to 47, means loving (*agapaō*) not only one's friends but one's enemies. "'Love your enemies and pray for those who persecute you, so that you may be sons of your Father who is in heaven'" (verses 44, 45). The parallel passage in Luke reinforces that message. "Be merciful," commands Jesus in the context of loving one's enemies (Luke 6:27-35), "even as your Father is merciful" (verse 36). Thus the Gospel writers equated being merciful with being perfect. Just as God sent Christ to die for His enemies (Rom. 5:6, 8, 10), so His children are to emulate His heart of love.

In commenting on Matthew 5:48, William Barclay nicely summarizes its message: "The one thing which makes us like God is the love which never ceases to care for men, no matter what men do to it. We...enter upon Christian perfection...when we learn to forgive as God forgives, and to love as God loves."[6]

The only other use of the word "perfection" in the Gospels is found in Christ's conversation with the rich young ruler. You will recall that in his desire to gain eternal life, the young man had come to Christ with a list of his commandment-keeping accomplishments. But he still felt that he had not done enough to gain the prize, so he asked Jesus what he still needed to do. The answer: "'If you would be perfect, go, sell what you possess and give to the poor, and you will have treasure in heaven; and come, follow me'" (Matt. 19:16-21).

Christ does not allow the young man to trivialize and itemize righteousness. Rather, He once again ties being perfect to loving one's neighbor, but He places that love in the context of a life-changing followership with Himself. "The real decision which Christ required from the rich young ruler," claims Hans LaRondelle, "was not primarily of an *ethical* [doing something] nature, but of a radical *religious* [relationship] nature: the complete self-surrender to God."[7] To relate to Christ includes assimilating and reflecting His character of love. A number of other Bible passages dealing with God's ideal for humans are in harmony with Jesus' Gospel statements on perfection (see, for example, 1 John 2:4-6; 4:7-12; James 1:27; Micah 6:8).

It is crucial at this juncture to realize that biblical perfection is a positive rather than a negative quality. The essence of perfection is not refraining from certain things and actions but of performing loving actions while in relationship to Christ. Perfection is reflected in daily living that demonstrates Christlike love toward both other people and God. "Perfection," writes Jean Zurcher, "is more than simply not doing wrong. It is the overcoming of evil with good in harmony with the basic principle laid down in the golden rule [of Matt. 7:12]."[8] "Character perfection," suggests C. Mervyn Maxwell, "is nothing less than to 'live love.'"[9]

Love, therefore, defines both SIN and Christian perfection. If, as we saw earlier, SIN is essentially focusing my love (*agapē*) on myself, the beginning of the pathway of biblical perfection is shifting that love back to God and my neighbor. That transformation, Paul indicates, will change every aspect of my everyday life (Rom. 13:8-10; Gal. 5:14).

Perfect love is not perfect performance, perfect skill, or perfect human nature. Rather, it is rendering obedience in relationship to both the God of love and the great principle undergirding His LAW. Attempts at "becoming perfect" divorced from a living relationship with Jesus and the loving heart of His

LAW are sterile, cold, dead, and often ugly—a truth frequently demonstrated by those of Pharisaic disposition.

It is now time to turn to the Bible words used to express the English word "perfection." None of them mean "sinlessness" or have absolutist connotations. The key New Testament word translated as "perfection" is *teleios*, the adjective form of *telos*. The idea behind *telos* has been brought into the English language in our word "teleology"—"the fact or quality of being directed toward a definite end or of having an ultimate purpose," according to Webster.

That meaning is from the Greek, in which *telos* means "an end," "a purpose," "an aim," or "a goal." Something is *teleios* if it fulfills the purpose for which it was created. People are therefore perfect (*teleios*) if they fulfill God's purpose for them. The Bible leaves no doubt as to the purpose for which humans are created. "'Let us make man in our image, after our likeness,'" reads the Genesis story (Gen. 1:26). It is only natural for Jesus to claim that the Christian ideal is that people should become *teleios* (perfect) in love, that they should become like their Father in heaven, who is loving at the core of His being (Matt. 5:43-48; 1 John 4:8). People are made to act in love rather than to behave like the devil.

The meaning of *teleios* is not "sinless" but "mature." Christ could therefore say to the rich young ruler that if he wanted to be perfect (*teleios*), he must become totally committed to God (Matt. 19:21). That means that he needed to be "mature" in his love to both God and other people. The mature commitment lies at the base of biblical perfection.

The idea of perfection as maturity is explicitly clear in Hebrews 5:13-6:1, where we read that Christians should move beyond the nourishing milk of their Christian childhood to the solid food of the "mature" (from *teleios*). The perfect are those who "go on to maturity" ("perfection," in the KJV, from *telos*).

The perceptive reader may have noted that when I began my discussion of biblical perfection in this chapter, nearly all my quotations were from the King James Version, contrary to my usual practice of using the Revised Standard Version. That was because the RSV (and other modern versions) nearly always translates the *telos* word group as "mature" rather than "perfect." It does so because that is what the word means.

According to the New Testament writers, the "perfect" Christian is the mature, whole, complete Christian. The same holds true for the Old Testament, where the words translated as "perfect" generally mean "complete," "upright," or "blameless" in a spiritual sense.

Thus Noah, Abraham, and Job could be called "perfect" (Gen. 6:9, KJV; 17:1, KJV; Job 1:1, 8, KJV), even though they had obvious faults. The perfect Old Testament saint was the person with the "perfect heart" toward God as he or she "walked" in His way and will (1 Kings 8:61, KJV; Isa. 38:3, KJV; Gen. 6:9; 17:1, KJV). The perfect person is the one in "total submission to the will of God" and in complete "devotion to His service"; the one who has "an unimpeded relationship with Yahweh."[10]

In summarizing the biblical view of perfection, it can be said that biblical perfection is not the abstract standard of flawlessness found in Greek philosophy but an individual's perfect relationship with God and his or her fellow humans. Biblical perfection involves ethical conduct, but it involves much more than mere behavior. It centers on maturing the relationships that were ruptured in the rebellion of the Genesis fall but are restored to individuals at conversion.

John Wesley's definitions of biblical perfection deserve more study than they often receive by Adventists. Perfection, he concluded, is perfect love of God and our neighbor expressed in word and action. And love to God is "to delight in him, to rejoice in his will, to desire continually to please him, to seek and find our happiness in him, and to thirst day and night for a fuller enjoyment of him."[11]

Again, Wesley wrote, perfection "is purity of intention, dedicating all the life to God. It is the giving God all our heart; it is one desire and design ruling all our tempers. It is the devoting, not a part, but all, our soul, body, and substance, to God. In another view, it is all the mind which was in Christ, enabling us to walk as Christ walked. It is the circumcision of the heart from all filthiness, all inward as well as outward pollution. It is a renewal of the heart in the whole image of God, the full likeness of Him that created it. In yet another, it is...loving God with all our heart, and our neighbor as ourselves." It is hard to improve on such a definition, one that Wesley saw as describing "the whole and sole perfection."[12]

Biblical sinlessness

The Bible explicitly teaches that we may be sinless in this life. The apostle John in his first epistle is clear on that point. "No one who abides in him sins.... No one born of God commits sin; for God's nature abides in him, and he cannot sin because he is born of God" (1 John 3:6, 9). "We know that whosoever is born of God sinneth not; but he that is begotten of God keepeth himself, and that wicked one toucheth him not" (5:18, KJV).

Taken by themselves, these passages appear to describe and require sinless perfection for every Christian. Yet other texts in this same epistle seem to imply just the opposite. For example, "if we say we have no sin, we deceive ourselves"; "if we confess our sins, he is faithful and just, and will forgive our sins"; "if we say we have not sinned, we make him a liar"; "I am writing this to you so that you may not sin; but if any one does sin, we have an advocate with the Father, Jesus Christ the righteous" (1:8-2:1).

In light of these two sets of texts, it is clear that John is either terribly confused or he is operating with a definition of sin that is more complex than is generally acknowledged by those who glibly quote him as saying that "sin is the transgression of the law" (3:4, KJV) and give that text an interpretation based purely on outward behavior.

The fact that John has a complex definition of sin in mind is evident not only from the passages quoted above but also from 1 John 5:16, where he notes that some sin is "not unto death," while other sin is "unto death" (KJV).

The faultline between that sin which cannot be found in the believer ("sins unto death," 3:9; 5:16) and those sins open to mediation by Christ ("not unto death," 1:9; 2:1) is found in a person's attitude. It is important to note that in all the passages in 1 John demanding sinlessness, the Greek verbs describing people who sin are in the present tense, thereby denoting people who live in a state of continual or habitual sinning. On the other hand, in 1 John 2:1, where we are told that if we sin we have a Mediator, the verb is in the aorist tense, indicating a definite action in a point of time. Thus the action is not ongoing and therefore is not habitual.

The picture in 1 John is the contrast between those who have an attitude of rebellion toward God and live in continual SIN as a way of life (i.e., have a SIN orientation rather than a FAITH orientation) and those who commit sins that they repent of as they turn to the Mediator for forgiveness and cleansing. The first category indicates those who have sinned "unto death," while the sin of those in the second category is "not unto death." Sins "unto death" are equivalent to the unpardonable sin of Matthew 12:31, 32. When people are in a state of rebellion and continuously reject the pleading of the Holy Spirit to repent of their sinful acts, they have placed themselves in a position to deny God's forgiving grace. Such rebellious hardness is the sin "unto death." It is impossible for a person to be a Christian and live in a state of SIN at the same time.

Those with SIN "unto death" live in a state of "lawlessness" (3:4) and rebellion toward God, while those in line with the Mediator have been "born of God," abide "in him," and have become a part of the family of God through adoption (3:9, 6, 1).

Because Christians have been born from above and have had their minds transformed, they do not have a rebellious attitude toward God. Rather, they "walk in the light, as he is in the light" (1:7; compare 2:6). On the other hand, some claiming to have "fellowship with him...walk in darkness" (1:6). "He who says 'I know him' but disobeys his commandments is a liar, and the truth is not in him" (2:4).

By his very use of the word "walk," it is clear that John is speaking of two ways of life that are in harmony with his use of verb tenses. We can walk with God or the devil. One way of life is the SIN relationship to God that leads to a life of ongoing law-lessness (sins) and ends in death. The other is the FAITH relationship, with its born-from-above attitude toward sin and its use of both the Mediator for cleansing and the Holy Spirit for empowerment. Those in this second group are defined by John as being sinless, even though they still commit acts of sin for which they need to be forgiven. Thus sinlessness is not only a possibility in the present life but a biblical promise and demand. The Christian "cannot sin [live in a state of rebellion] because he is born of God" (3:9). On the other hand, those not born of God "are the children of the devil." In their rebellion they neither do God's will, nor do they love their neighbor (3:10).

The distinction between sinlessness and absolute sinlessness is also found in Paul's conception of perfection and ultimate perfection. In Philippians he describes himself and some of the Philippians as already "perfect" (Phil. 3:15, KJV), yet in the same passage he claims that he had not yet attained to perfection (3:12, KJV). The "already-perfect" state refers to the Philippians' dedication of heart and mind to Christ, while the "not-yet-perfect" status suggests that Paul and his church were in a process of growth and development in their perfection. That is, they were already perfect (mature in their attitude to Christ), but they were on the way to a fuller perfection (maturity).

Thus, being perfect is a dynamic state in which dedicated Christians continue to advance in Christian living. Paul can therefore write to the Philippians that he is pressing on in his growing and developing perfection (3:12-14). His heart, mind, and attitude toward God were perfect and right, but he had not developed ultimate perfection. Paul could be perfect but not yet perfect in the same way that John's readers could be sinless but not yet sinless in the absolute sense. Bible readers too often pass over those scriptural distinctions.

Absolute sinlessness, when one begins to think about it, is a rather far-reaching state of being. Those who so glibly demand it of themselves and others usually define sin as merely avoiding conscious acts of rebellion against God. But sin also includes unconscious acts and acts of omission. In other words, absolute sinlessness (or absolute perfection) demands a complete forsaking of all conscious and unconscious sins, but it also requires that one never neglects doing good.

That distinction becomes especially pertinent when we note that the Pharisees of old were not condemned in Christ's portrayal of the final judgment for sins of commission but for sins of omission. That is, they failed the judgment, not because they had committed a sinful act, but because they had neglected to feed their neighbor and visit the sick (Matt. 25:31-46).

God's emphasis on the invisible sins of omission stands in stark contrast to those who would define sin only as consciously rebellious acts of commission. The standard of God's character is much higher than either modern or ancient Pharisees have taught. Of course, one good reason to lower the standard by defining sin only as conscious rebellion is that it makes it easier to reach. Thus, the negative approach of the Pharisaic mind is understandable.

Being "perfect" for Paul in Philippians and being "sinless" for John in his first epistle does not mean either absolute perfection or absolute sinlessness. But it does mean being free from an attitude of rebellion toward the Father and His principles set forth in the LAW of love.

Because of less-than-adequate bodies and flawed minds that don't know and understand everything (see 1 Cor. 13:12), even the most faithful Christians still commit sins of ignorance and sins of infirmity. As Wesley put it, there are those who "love God with all their heart.... But even these souls dwell in a shattered body, and are so pressed down thereby, that they cannot always exert themselves as they would, by thinking, speaking, and acting, precisely right. For want of better bodily organs, they must at times think, speak, or act wrong; not, indeed, through a defect of love, but through a defect of knowledge. And while this is the case, notwithstanding that defect, and its consequences, they fulfill the law of love," but not perfectly. Because of their shortfall of love in action, even though it is based upon ignorance and infirmity, they still "need the blood of atonement, and may properly for themselves...say, 'Forgive us our trespasses.'"[13]

Thus we can be perfect or sinless in attitude without being perfect or sinless in action. John, Paul, and Wesley agree on that point.

Paul's dichotomy between being already perfect but not yet perfect (Phil. 3:9-15) and John's division between being sinless but not yet sinless (1 John 3:9; 1:8-2:1; compare Rom. 6, 7) must be seen in terms of perfection of attitude versus perfection of action. The first should be the Christian's current possession; the second is an ideal aimed at in this life.

Perfection in the Bible, in terms of human beings in their mortal bodies, is perfection of the soul rather than total perfection in all its aspects. Thus the tension within Paul's perfect-but-not-yet-perfect teaching. The heart and mind have been transformed so that the Christian no longer has a willful desire or conscious intention to go on sinning. Christians are not slaves to sin (Rom. 6:18). Rather, they are servants of *agapē* love to both God and their fellow beings.

Because of that, it is possible, according to the Bible, for every Christian to live free from rebellion against God and His principles. Thus Jude writes that God is able to keep us "from falling" and "to present" us "without blemish before the presence of his glory" (Jude 24). As Ellen White put it, through God's help a person is enabled "to overcome every temptation wherewith he is beset."[14]

A major aspect of Christian perfection (or maturity) is the perfect desire to become perfect in love toward other people and God.

Please remember that Christian perfection is not merely entering into a conscious faith relationship in which wrong acts become repulsive; even more important, it is a reaching out in love to both God and one's fellow beings. Perfection is a life lived in outgoing love; it is a demonstration that the God of love has transformed both our hearts and our outward actions—two aspects of our lives that can never be separated. Thus Christian perfection is not merely negative (what I don't do) and internal; it is also positive (what I do do) and external. As a result, the Christian makes a difference in the quality of his or her world.

Points to ponder

1. My friend, you are paying the high price of success. You appear to be locked into completing an entire series on salvation to the local youth group. This week they want you to speak on perfection. In preparation, please develop a four-to-eight point outline (in full sentences) that will hit the high points and meet their needs.

2. List and briefly describe the various unbiblical approaches to perfection.

3. In four or five sentences, define the biblical approach to perfection. What is the relationship between perfection and sinlessness? How can a person be both perfect but not yet perfect?

4. Given the biblical definition of perfection, is running off to a "monastery" a good thing to do? Why or why not?

5. The apostle John has a complex definition of sin. How would you explain 1 John 3:9 to a mixed-up Christian? Please relate 1 John 3:9 to 1 John 1:8-2:1 and 5:16. Indicate the difference between those sins which are "unto death" and those sins which are "not unto death" (KJV).

Notes

1. Marvin Moore, *The Refiner's Fire* (Boise, ID: Pacific Press, 1990), 106, 107.

2. Ibid., 114.

3. John Wesley, *The Letters of the Rev. John Wesley, A.M.*, ed. John Telford (London: Epworth, 1931), 38.

4. For more on post-Millerite "spiritual wifery," see George R. Knight, *Millennial Fever and the End of the World: A Study of Millerite Adventism* (Boise, ID: Pacific Press, 1993), 251-257.

5. For more on holy flesh and Waggoner in this connection, see George R. Knight, *From 1888 to Apostasy: The Case of A. T. Jones* (Washington, DC: Review and Herald, 1987), 56-60; George R. Knight, *Angry Saints: Tensions and Possibilities in the Adventist Struggle over Righteousness by Faith* (Washington, DC: Review and Herald, 1989), 76.

6. Barclay, *Gospel of Matthew*, I:177.

7. Hans K. LaRondelle, *Perfection and Perfectionism: A Dogmatic-ethical Study of Biblical Perfection and Phenomenal Perfectionism* (Berrien Springs, MI: Andrews University Press, 1971), 181.

8. Jean R. Zurcher, *Christian Perfection: A Bible and Spirit of Prophecy Teaching* (Washington, DC: Review and Herald, 1967), 25.

9. C. Mervyn Maxwell, "Ready for His Appearing," in Herbert E. Douglass et al. *Perfection: The Impossible Possibility* (Nashville: Southern Publishing Assn., 1975), 164; cf. 141.

10. Paul Johannes Du Plessis, *Teleios: The Idea of Perfection in the New Testament* (Kampen, Netherlands: J. K. Kok [1959]), 241.

11. John Wesley, *The Works of John Wesley*, edited by Thomas Jackson, 3d ed. (Peabody, MA: Hendrickson, 1984), XI:446; VII:495.

12. John Wesley, *A Plain Account of Christian Perfection* (Kansas City, MO: Beacon Hill Press, 1966), 117, 118.

13. Ibid., 84.

14. White, *Selected Messages*, III:140.

CHAPTER SIX

I Used to Be Perfect

The most important thing you can know about me is that I used to be perfect. Notice the past tense—I *used* to be perfect. I used to be perfect in a way that I'm not perfect now.

Why was I perfect? I was perfect because I was a Seventh-day Adventist. I was perfect because Jesus was going to come, and in all sincerity,

- I wanted translation faith,
- I wanted translation character,
- I wanted translation perfection.

I was converted from agnosticism to Seventh-day Adventism at the age of nineteen. After becoming an Adventist, I looked around my church, its members, and its preachers, and I came to one conclusion. What a mess! You people had not pulled it off. I soon reasoned that you had failed in becoming perfect because you had not tried hard enough. I would be different. I would not fail. I would try harder than any of you had ever tried. At the time, I was working high construction steel out over San Francisco Bay. I still remember meditating on the problem one day high above the bay. It was then that I consciously decided and verbally committed myself to be the first perfect Christian since Christ—and I meant it. I was desperately sincere. But that thought gets ahead of my story.

The root of Adventism's fascination with perfection

The Adventist approach to being perfect really starts in the book of Revelation in the great texts in which Adventists have seen themselves and their movement pictured. The very focus of several of those texts seemingly points us toward behavior. "The dragon," we read, "was angry with the woman, and went off to make war on the rest of her offspring, on those who keep the commandments of God" (Rev. 12:17).

And then, of course, there is the Adventist interest in the great fourteenth chapter of Revelation. Note its progression. The first angel's message, initiated by William Miller in the 1830s and 1840s, points out that "the hour of his judgment has come" (verses 6, 7). The second angel's message pronouncing the fall of Babylon was begun in 1843 by Charles Fitch (verse 8). Then there is the crucial third message against worshiping the beast power. Adventists have especially focused on verse 12: "Here is a call for the endurance of the saints, those who keep the commandments of God and the faith of Jesus." That passage became the key text in Seventh-day Adventism. For nearly one hundred years, it was quoted in full under the masthead of every issue of the *Review and Herald*. Revelation 14 pictures that third message as the last before the return of Christ to "harvest" the earth (verses 14-20).

Early Seventh-day Adventists were good at preaching the first part of Revelation 14:12: "Here is the patience of the saints" (KJV). We saw ourselves in that verse as those who were still waiting for Jesus to come, in spite of the disappointment in 1844.

And we Adventists have loved the second part of 14:12: Here are "those who keep the commandments of God." Ah, I tell you, we Adventists have loved the commandments. If you take a look at the early Adventist writings (and some today), the emphasis when speaking on the twelfth verse was always on the word "keep." That is, by the way, a good emphasis in the context of a saving relationship with Christ. Here are "those who *keep* the commandments of God."

But early Adventists weren't quite sure what to do with "the faith of Jesus," the third part of Revelation 14:12. They interpreted "the faith of Jesus" to be a body of truth that was to be obeyed. As a result, our early writers—James White and nearly all the rest of them—said, in effect: "Well, God has His commandments, and Jesus has His commandments, such as foot washing, baptism, and so on." They developed a whole list of Jesus' commandments. As a result, Adventists became the "commandment commandment" people, focusing not only on God's commandments but on the commandments of Jesus as well. We were (and are) great doers.[1]

"The faith of Jesus" is the portion of Revelation 14:12 that Ellen White and others reinterpreted at the Minneapolis General Conference session in 1888 to emphasize "faith *in* Jesus."[2] The text can be translated as either "faith in Jesus" or "faith of Jesus." Many Seventh-day Adventists, reading the text as "faith of Jesus," have tended to imply that the verse is saying that because we have the "faith of Jesus" we can be just as absolutely sinless as He.

That interpretation has probably been encouraged by the first five verses of Revelation 14. Verse 1 reads: "Then I looked, and lo, on Mount Zion stood the Lamb, and with him a hundred and forty-four thousand who had his name and his Father's name written on their foreheads." And verses 4 and 5: "It is these who have not defiled themselves with women, for they are chaste; it is these who follow the Lamb wherever he goes"—not just part of the way, but all the way. "These have been redeemed from mankind as first fruits for God and the Lamb, and in their mouth no lie was found, for they are spotless." Now that's a pretty high standard. They are "spotless." Or as the King James Version puts it, "They are without fault before the throne of God." Now I'd call that perfect. It is not hard to see why many Seventh-day Adventists thought the way they did about the topic of perfection. After all, Revelation 12 and 14 are central texts to the denomination's identity.

Now we all know that we have a sort of perfection through justification by faith because we are in Christ. But these Revelation 14 texts raise the question, "Is justification by faith enough, or must we be sinlessly perfect in ourselves to be part of the 144,000?" And if there is something more than justification, what is it that must take place within us? That question has divided Seventh-day Adventism for a hundred years. What must happen in God's end-time people?

Before moving on, we should note the all-important flow of Revelation 14. We have the 144,000, the first angel, the second angel, the third angel, and immediately after the third angel the great second-coming drama—the harvest. In verses 14-15 we read: "Then I looked, and lo, a white cloud, and seated on the cloud one like a son of man, with a golden crown on his head, and a sharp sickle in his hand. And another angel came out of the temple, calling with a loud voice to him who sat upon the cloud, 'Put in your sickle, and reap, for the hour to reap has come, for the harvest of the earth is fully ripe.'"

Adventists have wanted sincerely to be ready for the coming of Jesus. And they not only have the Bible to urge them toward the concept of character perfection but also the writings of Ellen White. Here is one of her most impressive statements: "Christ is waiting with longing desire for the manifestation of Himself in His church. When the character of Christ shall be *perfectly reproduced* in His people, then He will come to claim them as His own."[3] The passage then immediately moves on to the harvest scene. In many ways this Ellen White passage parallels the progress and the flow of events in Revelation 14.

The key concept in that *Christ's Object Lessons* quotation is "perfectly reproduced." Unfortunately, when Seventh-day Adventists read such words as "perfectly reproduced," they tend to become somewhat emotional. I did when I first read them. I was carried away with both the magnificence and the possibility of the assignment and promise.

I don't know if you've ever seen anybody who is perfect. Sometimes I close my eyes and visualize some of the perfect people I have known. Here comes one now across the screen of my imagination. She is very satisfied because she has gotten the victory over cheese. Here comes another one. This one is a first-century Pharisee. This guy is really "religious." He knows exactly what size rock he can carry on the Sabbath day and how far he can carry it without carrying a burden and thus committing sin. He has shaved righteousness down to some very slim slivers of "religion." He is convinced that with such dedication to lifestyle detail, he will soon be perfect.

Then there are those who seem to be perfect through health reform. In one little Adventist church of thirty members, there is an elder who is willing to take communion service to shut-ins. But he will not partake of the emblems with them, because that would be eating between meals. I wonder what "communion" means to such an elder?

The same congregation has a man six feet, five inches tall who weighs only 130 pounds. He has achieved tremendous dietary victories as he has moved toward being "perfect like Christ." He has even convinced himself that it is wrong to eat grains such as wheat and oats. As a result, unfortunately, he finds himself lusting for strange things. Every Wednesday he "falls" and eats two puffed-rice patties. This man, in his own eyes, is moving along the track to "real perfection." When a person is down to two puffed-rice patties a week as his most "sinful activity," he must be getting somewhere. Such a one must be almost perfect, at least along one line of "perfection."

There is another saint in this same little church who had an injury. For a normal person, it would have taken three weeks to heal. But this "health reformer" still wasn't healed after six weeks because of dietary deficiencies. Such was the fruit of her health reform. Ellen White labeled such dedication in her day as "health deform."[4]

Some Seventh-day Adventists have gone in strange directions in their quest for character perfection. Perhaps that is because some of us don't have the slightest idea what character is. Nor do we have the foggiest notion what Ellen White meant by Christ's character.

My road to perfection

The *Christ's Object Lessons* passage I quoted above had a large impact on my own Adventist experience. Soon after I became a Seventh-day Adventist, some dear saint showed me that passage. And it was after reading that Christ would come after His character had been perfectly reproduced in His children that I consciously decided I would be the first perfect Christian since Christ. I immediately set out on my quest.

As a result, within a few weeks, I could tell what was wrong with almost everything.

- I could tell you what was *wrong* with anything you might want to eat.
- I could tell you what was *wrong* with anything you might want to watch.
- I could tell you what was *wrong* with almost anything you might want to do.
- And I could tell you what was *wrong* with almost anything you might want to think.

I became an expert at pointing out the wrong in everybody and everything. In my own rigorous approach to diet, I went from 165 pounds to roughly 123 pounds in about three months.

Some feared that I would die of "health reform."

And I want you to know something. In my striving to become perfect, I became perfect.

- I was the perfect Pharisee after the order of Saul before he met Jesus on the Damascus road.
- I was the perfect monk after the order of Martin Luther before he discovered the gospel in Romans.
- I was the perfect Methodist after the order of the struggling, striving John Wesley before his Aldersgate conversion experience.

As I later discovered, my path to perfection had been well-trod before me.

That brings me to the paradox of perfection. Those of you who know someone "perfect" will recognize the paradox. Some of you will have lived through it, and in most congregations I find people still living through it, or, worse yet, people trying to exist with someone who is living through it.

The paradox of my perfection was that the more I thought about my perfection, the more self-centered I became. Not only did I become self-centered, but the more I strove and the more I tried, the more judgmental I became toward those who had not achieved my "high level." Not only was I judgmental, but the more "perfect" I became, the harsher I was with others who had not equaled my "superior status" and the more negative I became about the church and others who were not as "pure" or "dedicated" as I.

In short, the harder I tried, the worse I got. That was the paradox of my perfection. *In my route to perfectly reproducing the character of Christ, I had more closely mirrored the character of the devil.* To say the least, I became a difficult person to live with. People became a problem in my life as I sought to emulate the character of the Saviour. After all, people got in the way of my dietary rigor. And they interfered with my thoughtful hour of meditating upon Christ each day. People hampered my reaching out for perfection.

Unfortunately, there is a way of perfection that leads to the very self-centeredness of SIN itself. There is a way to perfection that is the way of death. There is a way to perfection that is destructive, and too many Adventists have taken that route to supposedly reproducing the character of Christ. It is the wrong road. It is the way of humanity rather than God's way.

In my frustration with my church and myself, I turned in my ministerial credentials. But my conference president, seeing my bewilderment and wanting to "save me for the work," had me drive three hundred miles so that he could counsel with me, encourage me, and return my credentials. I couldn't get rid of them. I turned them in a second time, and they came back again. The third time, I wrote a strongly worded letter telling my conference president exactly how I felt. That did the trick. The credentials did not come back.

I was finished as an Adventist minister. As far as I was concerned, I was finished as both an Adventist and a Christian. For six years I did not pray or read the Bible, unless I was forced into it in public. I studied philosophy to find a better answer to the meaning in life, only to find it bankrupt in terms of real answers. Near the end of my years in a "far country," I came to the conclusion that if Christianity didn't have the answer, there was no answer. That was one of the most frightening conclusions of my life.

Then early in 1975 God reached down and touched me. He said in effect, "George, you've been an Adventist, but you haven't been a Christian. You've known all the doctrines, but you haven't known Me." At that point, I went through my own 1888 crisis. I met Jesus, and my Adventism got baptized into Christianity.

The tragedy of the matter for me, those who had to live with me, and those like me, is that many of these situations could have been prevented had we been more faithful in our reading of inspired statements. Had I just read the context to many of the statements that drove me on, I would have been saved from some of the most costly mistakes in my life.

God's road to PERFECTION

Too often, we've done violence to both the writings of Ellen White and the Bible. One way we do this is by not reading statements in context. We rip quotations out of context, such as the one in *Christ's Object Lessons* on perfectly reproducing the character of Christ. Then we go to such books as *Counsels on Diet and Foods* or *Messages to Young People*, and we rip out a bunch more quotations. We next connect them with the *Christ's Object Lessons* passage in such a way as to create a theology that even God can't figure out.

Always read the context.[5] Find out what the inspired author is saying, whether that author be Paul or Peter or John or Ellen White. What a difference in our understanding and in our lives the context can make! For example, let us take a look at the context of our statement from *Christ's Object Lessons* on perfectly reproducing the character of Christ. In the immediately preceding paragraphs we read: "Christ is seeking to reproduce Himself in the hearts of men; and He does this through those who believe in Him. The object of the Christian life is fruit bearing—the reproduction of Christ's character in the believer, that it may be reproduced in others....

"There can be no growth or fruitfulness in the life that is centered in self. If you have accepted Christ as a personal Saviour, you are to forget yourself, and try to help others. Talk of the love of Christ, tell of His goodness. Do every duty that presents itself. Carry the burden of souls upon your heart.... As you receive the Spirit of Christ—the Spirit of unselfish love and labor for others—you will grow and bring forth fruit. The graces of the Spirit will ripen in your character. Your faith will increase, your convictions deepen, *your love be made perfect.* More and more you will reflect the likeness of Christ in all that is pure, noble, and lovely."[6]

The next few lines contain the statement that "when the character of Christ shall be perfectly reproduced in His people, then He will come to claim them as His own."[7] *Perfectly reproducing the character of Christ is reflecting His love.* The character of Christ centers in the caring relationship.

Too often, Adventists have looked at religion as a negative, but Christianity is not what we don't do. No one will ever be saved by what he or she avoided. Christianity is a positive rather than a negative. True Christianity is a religion that frees us from preoccupation with ourselves and struggling to earn our salvation so that we can truly love our neighbor, our God, our brother, our wife, our husband, our children, and so on.

That was the great message of Jesus. "Be ye therefore perfect," He proclaimed, "even as your Father which is in heaven is perfect" (Matt. 5:48, KJV). Remove that text from its context, and you can make it into something the Bible never said. Read it in its context, and you will discover what Jesus was trying to teach. Beginning in verse 43, our passage teaches that God loves everyone. He makes the rain to fall and the sun to shine on both good and evil people, on both the just and the unjust. Jesus is telling us that we are to be perfect or mature in love to others even as our "heavenly Father is perfect" in His love to us. Please remember that Christ died for you while you were still His enemy (Rom. 5:6, 10). To be like the Father, we must also love our enemies (Matt. 5:43-48).

Can you love like God loved? That is Christian maturity or Christian perfection. And if you don't believe it, compare Matthew 5:48 with Luke 6:36. Luke 6:27-36 is the third Gospel's parallel passage to Matthew 5:43-48. Both deal with loving one's enemies, and both conclude with the injunction that Christians are to be like God. But Luke's passage does not say, "Be ye therefore perfect," but, "Be ye therefore merciful, as your Father also is merciful" (Luke 6:36, KJV). The evangelists equated the saying of Christ on perfection with mercy.

For more insight on this topic, we need to turn to Matthew 25:31-46 and the great judgment scene of the sheep and the goats. That is a fantastic passage. Read it today for yourself, and count the question marks. Note the great surprise that is experienced in the judgment. On the one hand, Jesus says to one group: "Enter into My kingdom."

According to the parable, they say, "Lord, how did we make it? We're not like those Pharisees. We didn't spend all our life worrying about the multitude of dos and don'ts."

Jesus replies, "You don't understand. When I was hungry, you fed Me. When I was in prison, you visited Me. And when I was thirsty, you gave Me drink."

They query in return, "Wait a minute. How can that be? We never saw You or fed You."

"But," Jesus answers, "if you did it unto one of the least of these my brothers, you did it to Me."

About this time the other group is really getting excited. There are quite a few Pharisees in this second group—individuals who have dedicated their entire lives to observing the multitude of the bits and pieces of the law. "Wait a second, Lord," they cry out; "we kept the Sabbath. We really kept the Sabbath. We had some 1,500 laws and rules and regulations regarding the Sabbath, and we kept them all. We knew exactly where the lines were. And we not only kept the Sabbath; we paid tithe rigorously. We were so scrupulous that we tithed every tenth leaf from our little mint plants. And we had a good diet. Lord, You have to save us. We deserve it."

"Well," replies Jesus, "there is only one problem. When I was in prison, you didn't seem to care. When I was hungry, where were you?"

"Lord," they shoot back, "if we had known it was You, we would have been right down there."

"But," Jesus responds, "you haven't gotten the point. You have not internalized the principle of My kingdom. You have not internalized the great principle of love. And if you don't have that, you will not be happy in My kingdom."

Matthew 25 is very explicit on the fact that the judgment turns upon one point. But if you need more help, try The *Desire of Ages*. Ellen White says it as plainly as words can put it. "Thus," she writes after citing Matthew 25, "Christ on the Mount of Olives pictured to His disciples the scene of the great judgment day. And He represented its *decision as turning upon one point*. When the nations are gathered before Him, there will be but two classes, and their eternal destiny will be determined by what they have done or have neglected to do for Him in the person of the poor and the suffering."[8]

If people are not passing on the love of God to their neighbors, it is because they don't have it. If people have God's love in their hearts, there is no way it can be kept corked up. It will find expression. The expression of God's love to those whom Jesus loves is the great criteria in the great final judgment. God wants everyone to be in heaven who will be happy there. And those who will be happy will be those who have given up the principle of self-love and self-sufficiency (SIN) and have let God infuse the great principle of His LAW into their hearts and lives. The new birth includes the shift in a person's life from selfishness and self-centeredness (SIN) to other-centeredness and love for others (the principle of the LAW). Sanctification is merely the process of becoming more loving. The biblical picture of perfection is becoming mature in expressing God's love. Such people are forming characters like Christ's, for "God is love" (1 John 4:8). Such people are safe to save for eternity.

God's final demonstration to the universe

That thought brings us to the topic of God's final demonstration to the universe. In *Christ's Object Lessons*, we read that "the last message of mercy to be given to the world, is a revelation of His character of love."[9] The final demonstration to the universe of what grace can do in human lives will be a revelation of God's success in transforming selfish individuals into lovers of God and humankind. The final demonstration is not one portraying a people who finally get the victory over peanut butter, cheese, or other items of diet, or, for that matter, behavior in general. The great demonstration to the universe deals with the reproduction of the character of Christ.

One of the great texts of the New Testament gets at the heart of the matter. "By this," said Jesus, "all men will know that you are my disciples," if you keep the Sabbath. "By this all men will know that you are my disciples," if you pay tithe. "By this all men will know that you are my disciples," if you have the proper diet.

Too many Adventists have read the New Testament as if it said those types of things. But Jesus actually said, "By this all men will know that you are my disciples, if you have love for one another" (John 13:35). Love is not only the one point on which the judgment turns; it is also the point by which Jesus identifies His disciples. To be a follower of Christ is to be a lover of God and our fellow beings.

Too many Seventh-day Adventists have missed that central New Testament teaching. Too many have the rules, regulations, and laws (which do have a proper place in the context of a saving relationship with Jesus) but have missed the great principle that forms the foundation of God's LAW. Too many, in their striving for perfection, work at the level of sins and laws rather than letting God work in them at the level of SIN and LAW. Unfortunately, all the rules and regulations without the love of Jesus make for mighty dreary religion—or worse yet, destructive religion.

When I go to camp meeting, I can look out on an audience of ten thousand people and spot the so-called "perfect" ones at a glance. They are the ones who aren't smiling. They are the ones who apparently have nothing to celebrate and rejoice in because they do not have assurance in Christ.

Now if I were the devil, I would give you Adventists Bible truth, but I would make you and your churches colder than cucumbers in a Montana blizzard. On the other hand, I would give some Christians joy in church and in their Christian lives, but I would mix up their theology so badly that they couldn't tell Genesis from Revelation.

What Adventists need is the joy of salvation combined with their great doctrinal truths. When Adventists have both Jesus in their hearts and assurance of salvation, they will not only have the truth with a small t (that is, doctrinal truth), but they'll have TRUTH with a capital T (the Lord of Truth). "I am...the truth," said Jesus (John 14:6).

I am personally convinced that the great thing needed to get Adventism on the move is not only doctrinal truth, but a better knowledge of Jesus and the beautiful assurance of salvation in Him. We need both truth and TRUTH. When Adventists have both, it will show forth from every part of their beings and in their worship, and they will be in a position to let the Holy Spirit use them to move the world with their beautiful MESSAGE.

Points to ponder

1. Good news! You have only one more talk to prepare for the local youth group. It's not that they are tired of you, but their leaders have developed a program that will get them into the community in service and witnessing programs for the next few weeks. Meanwhile, for your last presentation they want you to discuss the meaning of Matthew 5:48 and *Christ's Object Lessons* page 69 in their context. In two brief paragraphs, jot down the essential information for each of those passages that you can use to guide your presentation.

2. List and describe the main passages in the book of Revelation that have led Adventists to be concerned with perfection. What has made those texts so forceful in the minds of many Adventists?

3. Write a paragraph on the "paradox of perfection" that deals with why it is that the harder people try to achieve

perfection the worse they become. Be sure to include in your discussion how the paradox relates to SIN and LAW.

4. Utilizing the categories of SIN and LAW, discuss the importance of God's "final demonstration to the universe."

Notes

1. For treatments of Adventism's traditional understanding of Revelation 14:12, see Knight, *Angry Saints*, 53-55; Knight, *A User-Friendly Guide*, 105, 106.

2. For examinations of the reinterpretation of Revelation 14:12, see Knight, *Angry Saints*, 55-60; Knight, *A User-Friendly Guide*, 106-110.

3. White, *Christ's Object Lessons*, 69 (italics supplied).

4. Ellen G. White to Bro. and Sis. Kress, May 29, 1901, published in Ellen G. White, *Counsels on Diet and Foods* (Washington, DC: Review and Herald, 1976), 202.

5. For more on the principles of reading Ellen White's writings, see George R. Knight, *Reading Ellen White: How to Understand and Apply Her Writings* (Hagerstown, MD: Review and Herald, 1997).

6. White, *Christ's Object Lessons*, 67, 68 (italics supplied).

7. Ibid., 69.

8. White, *Desire of Ages*, 637 (italics supplied).

9. White, *Christ's Object Lessons*, 415.

Index of Biblical References

Index of Names and Topics

RIGHTEOUSNESS, defined, 22; related to righteous actions, 22

Ruler, rich young, 31, 32, 34, 74, 75

Sabbath, 36, 37

Saint, 46

Salvation, related to SIN, 20, 21, 27; unity of, 22, 52-54

Sanctification, a unity, 48, 52-54; characteristics of, 48-52; defined, 46, 49, 65, 96; progressive, 48, 51, 70; versus justification, 41, 42, 52, 53; work of a lifetime, 48; work of a moment, 44, 46, 47

Satan, 27; mode of attack, 14; tempted Christ, 62-63

Selected Messages, 34, 35

Sermon on the Mount, 35, 49

Seventh-day Adventists, and law, 25, 26; and perfection, 85-90

Sin, complexity of definition, 77, 78, 80

SIN, as a power, 19, 20; as nakedness, 15, 16; as rebellion, 19, 63, 78, 79, 80; atomization of, 31; characteristics of, 17, 19; defined by Jesus, 18, 19; definition of, 13, 15, 18, 44; earth's first, 13-18; relation of sin to, 15, 18, 79; relational concept, 19, 23, 79; results of, 15-17; sets the

stage for understanding of salvation, 20, 21

Sinful acts versus sinful nature, 19, 20

Sinless, biblical, 77-82

Sinlessness, 67

Sins of omission, 80

Surrender, 52

Temptation, ours, 63-65

TEMPTATION, Christ's, 59-63, 65; defined, 58-61, 66; relation to temptations, 57, 67

Ten Commandments, related to the LAW, 29, 30, 35, 38, 39

Vick, Edward, 19

Vindication, the purpose of the judgment, 54, 55

Waggoner, E. J., 71

Wesley, John, on perfection, 5, 71, 76, 77, 81, 91

White, Ellen, 26, 27, 37, 82, 87, 90; on LAW, 27, 35; on sin, 20; on perfection, 88, 93; on the will, 64

White, James, 87

Will, Christ's, 62; human, 64-66

Works, 50, 51

Zurcher, Jean, 74